ÓRGIVA

A CHANCER'S GUIDE TO RURAL SPAIN

First Published in Great Britain 2020 by Cabra Publishing

First edition: 2020

ISBN: 9798615021855

Cabra Publications.
10 Town Meadow.
Little Torrington.
Torrington. Devon.
EX38 8RD.

ÓRGIVA

A Chancer's Guide to Rural Spain

Andy Bailey

Dedication

To the other Chancer's.
Sarah my wife and Alex my daughter.
Team effort.

Preface

DO YOU GAMBLE? MOST PEOPLE DO. Horse racing, lotteries, bingo, the stock market, cards. Attempting the second run at cricket when you know you can't make it. It's even easier to gamble these days with the smartphone at your fingertips and every betting company tempting you with special sign up offers. My father, who was an accountant would never gamble. I'd say, "Let's have a punt on the Grand National?"

"Waste of money," he'd reply.

But he did gamble. He ploughed a lot of money each month into his private pension fund and so did his employer. His national insurance contributions were also a gamble, ask the generation of women who now won't receive their pension until they are sixty-seven. He gambled each time he opened a packet of his beloved Senior Service tipped. He lost out on both. He died of cancer only two years into his retirement. My mother, a qualified state-registered nurse and midwife should have benefited from the widow's side of the pension, but she died two years later also of cancer. Players No. 6 got her.

Gambling is not just a financial thing, it's a life choice as well. Moving out of the comfort zone.

So, moving to Spain in the year 2000 with my wife, Sarah and six-year-old daughter, Alex seemed like a gamble worth taking. Our friends and family (what were left of them) hailed our decision as brave. "It's only Europe," was our reply.

This book, *ÓRGIVA: A Chancer's Guide to Rural Spain*, is an account of our years of experience of life in rural Spain. The tribulations, the frustrations, our struggle with the language, the happy times, and the tragic times but also the relative success in a country we never envisaged living in or loving so much. The chapters are in no specific order but what I hope they will do is provide advice and information for any others who may be considering a similar gamble and bring a smile to your face as I recount the various events that have tripped us up but learnt from over the years. The secret to success is to minimise the risk and of course, lots of luck.

Every region, province, town and village in Spain has its own way of running things. My experience and advice cannot relate to every part of Spain, and laws can also change without much notice at all.

Contents

Órgiva

THE SKY WAS THE COLOUR OF a Manchester City football shirt and the almond blossom reminded me of those cotton wool balls women remove their make-up with (and blokes I suppose). Every hue of pinks and whites possible. The mountains of the Sierra Nevada had a blanket of snow on them which seemed to enhance all the colours around us.

What a stunning introduction to the Alpujarras. It was the middle of February and we were making our first visit to mainland Spain. Having left the doom and gloom of England behind, the temperature here was a pleasant sixteen degrees and the holiday was off to a good start. And that's all it was, a holiday. Our accommodation for the week was a self-catering casita (small house) on the Tijola road out of Órgiva in Andalucia.

On the way to our casita we drove over some lemons and with some luck found our abode. What a beautiful place, nestled in a valley with views across the Rio Guadalfeo (ugly river) to the mountains of the Contraviesa and the hippy camp of Cigarones.

Once settled in, and with our six-year-old daughter, Alex looking expectantly at the swimming pool, we noticed our casita had nothing in stock. None of the basics like toilet paper, salt, pepper, olive oil (which could be purchased off the owners) washing-up liquid, beer etc.

Sarah exclaimed, "If we had letting houses, they would at least have a welcoming pack."

Alarm bells should have started ringing!

Well, off we went into town to purchase all the necessary supplies. There were lots of bars and restaurants, mainly all with the same menu, supermarkets, five banks, no charity shops and no estate agents. Not that we were looking for estate agents, just curious.

You could spot us a mile away in our shorts and sandals, we were in holiday mode. While in the town we had a beer in Nemesis One. There must be a Nemesis Two somewhere? Every time we had a drink the landlord brought us a tasty morsel.

Ah, we thought, *this must be tapas.*

The Granada province is one of the last areas to serve tapas with beer, wine or musto (non-alcoholic wine). Not with spirits or soft drinks though. The townspeople were well wrapped up, but to us it was like an August day back in England.

It was not long before Alex was enjoying the pool. It was a little fresh and she tried in vain to coax us in. No chance, it's February. Living in a rural area in England we thought we had fresh air but here we noticed how pure the air was and how well we slept. The shutters on the windows kept out the early morning light.

Our hosts were people we had known back in Somerset where they used to run the local pub. They had moved to Órgiva to be close to their granddaughter and had bought a ruin to convert into letting houses and what a great job they had done. The garden was well stocked with colourful plants, oranges and lemons providing bright orbs of sunshine and slices of fruit for our liquid refreshments.

During the holiday it was carnival time in Órgiva, normally eight weeks before Easter but the celebrations had to be spread over many weekends as only one marquee was available in the area for so many towns and villages. Friday night was the kids' turn and we managed to get Alex dressed up as a clown. It was good to get involved and we could feel the warmth and friendliness of the local parents with children of a similar age. Saturday was for the adults.

Órgiva is the capital market town of the Alpujarras with a population of around five thousand people. It's a bustling busy town with a very cosmopolitan, bohemian atmosphere. Mining and agriculture are its main activities but with tourism catching on. The ski resort of the Sierra Nevada is only an hour and a half away and the beaches of Motril and Salobreña just forty minutes down the road. At four hundred and fifty metres above sea level the town has a micro climate in which many different crops can grow, all fed from the waters of the melting snow off the mountains.

While settling into our holiday routine and thoroughly enjoying our surroundings a niggling question was emerging from somewhere in the back of my mind. What's the price of property around here? And could we do what our hosts had achieved?

I needed to find an estate agent. These elusive characters operated in pairs, one foreign and one local. I was told they hung around a coffee bar called Galindos, and coffee time and breakfast time was at ten. So off I set to track them down.

My luck was in and I found a guy called Dharmo and his Spanish mate, Ramon (Dharmo's corredor). Dharmo made the contacts with the foreigners and Ramon found the properties.

On introducing myself I was eyed with suspicion; they were in no hurry to show me their portfolio of property. Eventually Dharmo pulled out of his well-worn satchel a photograph album with pictures of ruins of farmhouses, town houses and bare parcels of land. But no prices.

I explained my idea and a ballpark figure of our budget. The mood lightened and they were sure they could find something suitable. Not wanting to get their hopes up I told them this was our first visit to the area, and we would have to return later in the year with funds and a plan. Numbers were exchanged and off I went with a feeling of dizziness. The road to Tijola is not the safest and with my attention elsewhere I was lucky not to end up in the irrigation channel (acequia).

Before our holiday we had sold our smart four-bedroom detached property in Evercreech, Somerset and bought a smaller detached house in the same village that needed a lot of work doing to it, but in the mean time we had paid off our mortgage.

To be in our early forties and in this position was a strange feeling. I was working as a dairy hygiene and mastitis consultant (sales rep) achieving my targets and not getting paid much, driving a thousand miles a week and putting on weight.

Sarah was caring for our six-year-old daughter and fitting in cleaning jobs where she could. At weekends I would milk cows so my farmer friends could have a day off. We had considered looking at bed and breakfast businesses in the Evercreech area as the Bath and West showground was close and held events most weekends. But with all the red tape and regulations this was a risky option.

On arriving back at the casita, Sarah asked what I had been up to. "Oh, nothing much," I replied, thinking I would leave it until later when a gin or two might have helped soften her up before suggesting my plan. So later that day under the shade of an olive tree and a gin and tonic in hand I steered the subject around to the possibility of us moving to this part of the world and running our own letting business. Expecting a negative reply, to my amazement I got a positive, she had already thought about that and we should investigate property prices and locations.

It was only three days into our holiday and major decisions were being discussed about the family's future. Discussing the possible options with various people they all agreed that moving a six-year-old child from England to Spain would not be a problem. It's when they are in their teens it's difficult. At Alex's age kids are like sponges and pick up a new language easily, unlike their parents! So, we reserved a two-week holiday in the coming June with our hosts and cancelled our holiday in France, where we always holidayed but never dreamt of moving there. As we always said about France: 'fantastic food, great wine, brilliant countryside but the people'.

It's strange how you get a feeling about a life changing situation in such a short time. Taking off from Malaga with the sky as blue as ever my daughter said, "Look at all those sheep." She was referring to the whitewashed houses on the mountain side. Still, it made a few people laugh.

Getting back to England and trying to keep a secret is quite tricky, with nothing tangible but an idea and so much to organise. First it was off to the building society. Pat the manageress was quite confused. "You have just paid it off what on earth do you want another one for?" She was quite a close friend, so I explained our plan. "Where in Spain?"

I told her she would not have heard of the place. Wrong. She had been there on a Yoga holiday. Well blow me down with a feather. The forms were signed, and we had our mortgage back. Hopefully enough for our adventure. Next the house needed renovating, quickly. Both of us being experienced with such matters, we soon had things moving along. In eight weeks, the place was looking a lot different. The idea was to rent it out until we were sure the move was right for all of us. Don't burn your bridges!

We decided to drive down to Spain as I had the use of the company car, so the ferry was booked for a Friday which meant skipping off work a day early. A couple of miles out to sea and my phone rang, it was my boss. "Can we meet up for lunch?" That would be a bit difficult I explained. "I want to see you when you get back."

I thought, *If I ever come back.*

The drive through France was fine and after a night's stop on the east coast of Spain we arrived back in Órgiva all excited and ready to start house hunting. It was the second week in June and the weather was warming up. It's good to get a contrast of seasons before you make the move.

Dharmo had been expecting us and had some property he thought would be suitable. First a massive old farmhouse on the Tijola road, with lots of land. My dream come true, a farm owner at last. The second was in Byacas, again a nice property, with land, good situation but the room above the property was owned by a relative from

Barcelona. He was not selling. The third was on the Camino de Pago a much more inviting area with views to the Lugar and the Sierra Nevada and close to town.

"That's enough for one day," Sarah exclaimed.

Over supper, each of the day's viewing were dismissed. The Tijola one had too much to be done and the land would be a distraction to our plan and that road is so dangerous. The second, we did not want some chap turning up for his annual holiday in August when we should be full of paying guests. The third was in the right location but too small.

The next day Dharmo and Ramon took us to a property on the Camino la Estrella. Part of the approach road was being resurfaced so we had a bit of a detour, ending up close to where we were the day before. Dharmo explained this property had just come on the market and was owned by an English lady, and it had been run as a letting business for a number of years. It consisted of three casitas (small houses) set in a wonderful garden and had a small pool. Our eyes lit up and our imagination took over. Not seeming to be too keen we asked the price: twenty-two million pesetas. Doing my best impersonation of one of the farmers I deal with, I took a deep intake of air through my teeth. I acted the bad cop whilst Sarah played the good cop.

"Would she accept twenty million?" I asked. "We are ready to go; we have the money and could complete in six weeks."

After some discussion between Dharmo and the lady owner, a deal was struck. So, after two days of house hunting, we hit the jackpot. Next, we had to go to Motril to get our NIE numbers, national identity number. In those days you had your thumb print taken and a photo and in return you received a laminated identity card, all for five thousand pesetas. (You cannot purchase any property or anything else of importance in Spain without this number.) Then it was off to the bank to open an account.

This all seems to be too simple, I thought, but with expert guidance from Dharmo within the week the pre-contract (compra venta) was signed and a deposit paid. The biggest gamble yet.

In this contract both parties agree the terms of the purchase, the deposit, the time scale, what's being included in the sale, possible harvesting of crops after the sale, etc. It's to protect both parties. Before you get this far a credit and debt check on the property is needed. This is called a nota-simple and anybody can obtain one of these, you do not need to be the property owner.

The purchase of our future being achieved so quickly meant we had time to explore. A day at the Alhambra Palace in Granada left us mesmerized and in awe. The most visited tourist site in Spain and we had just bought a tourist business just an hour down the road. The beaches on the Costa Tropical Salobreña, Almuñécar and La Herradura were not quite up to the standard of the beaches of Cornwall where I grew up but then they are not on the Mediterranean. No wetsuit needed here.

We took a drive up to the ski resort, two thousand metres above sea level, rising to three thousand three hundred metres. (Ben Nevis is one thousand three hundred and forty-five metres.) With all the snow melted the green pastures and mountain flowers were in full bloom. Sheep grazed peacefully on the slopes where only a few months ago people sped down with skis and snowboards attached to their limbs. A line of horses passed by on a trek. Granada lay below in a summer haze and the Mediterranean glistened in the distance.

"It's a little bit different than Somerset," my daughter exclaimed. "Can I learn to ski? What about horse riding as well?"

"I think Alex is quite keen," I whispered to Sarah.

On the eve of San Juan, twenty-third of June in Lanjaron, a massive water fight takes place in the high street. This is to celebrate Saint John the Baptist. We were told it's quite a spectacle, so off we went with Alex and her friend Amber (coincidentally a mate from Somerset). We got absolutely drenched and even with a change of clothes our teeth would not stop chattering and the girls were getting upset so we headed back to Órgiva.

It was time to leave Órgiva our new adopted home and head back to

St. Malo for the ferry. The plan was to return in the middle of August to complete the purchase, move in and get Alex settled before school started in early September. I remember during the ferry crossing we bored the pants off a couple sitting near us about our news, we had to tell someone.

Oh, When the Saints

SAINT'S DAYS ARE AN IMPORTANT PART of Spanish life. Each region, city, town and village have its own patron saints, all celebrated with fiestas, church services, noisy fireworks and explosions. During this book I will describe in calendar order the saints who are celebrated in and around Orgiva. I must emphasise that the celebrations are often moved to the nearest weekend from the actual feast day and the order of the celebration can change without notice. Imagine myself explaining to a newcomer the order of proceedings with great authority and then it's completely different from the year before.

Saint Anton Abad:
January 17th

SAN ANTON ABAD. ANTHONY THE GREAT. Patron of: Basket makers, brush makers, butchers, domestic animals, grave diggers, herdsmen and swine.

San Anton or Saint Anthony the Great was from Egypt and lived to the ripe old age of one hundred and five. 12/1/251 to 17/1/356. It is believed he was the first Christian monk and so is regarded as the father of all monks. San Anton the Abbot. He was a hermit for most of his life living in caves, fighting with the devil. Anthony's special gift was to cure infectious diseases particularly of the skin. Shingles can be referred to St. Anthony's fire. As patron saint to domestic animals, his feast day is the only day in the Catholic Church that animals are allowed into the Church to be blessed, apart from the odd donkey near Easter.

Horse shows and parades are held all over Spain during the week before his feast day.

San Anton is the patron saint of Torviscon, a village about eight kilometres upriver of Orgiva. This fiesta is completely nuts; fires (hogueras) are lit on important crossroads in the village at about 9.00pm, burning broom collected from the mountains. This burns very hot and with lots of crackle. The fires are extremely welcome as a January night can be bitter. Don't wear your best coat though as the sparks can ruin your ermine. But you can have with you the red piece of underwear you wore on New Year's Eve to throw into the fire for good luck. It is known as the night of the spark (chispa). It is also the only day in our locality that you can have a bonfire without permission.

Rockets are let off during the whole evening, with the locals firing them out of their hand. (Don't try this at home.) When the fires die down and the supply of broom has been exhausted pork is cooked on the embers. The village will have a couple of free-roaming pigs they feed during the year on scraps and then they get put to the knife before the fiesta. Don't forget San Anton is the patron of swine! Knock off the S and you have wine, gallons of the stuff, made by the locals from the product of the vines of the Contraviesa. Now this wine is called costa, it's innocuous in appearance, very moreish and lethal! I have seen it poured out of adapted beer barrels, plastic bottles, a fountain and from a model of the church with a tap on the steeple. On our first visit to this fiesta we sampled enough, on our latest visit and now knowing a lot of the locals it was difficult to pass a fire by without getting another glass of costa thrust into our hand. We had arranged a taxi home thankfully.

In a neighbouring hamlet, Notas, they also celebrate San Anton. A massive bonfire is built in the tiny plaza. A friend who lives there could not believe the locals had all their windows open as well as the church doors, all the smoke and ashes entering the buildings.

She asked an old Spanish lady politely in her best local dialect, "Are the windows and doors open to let the evil spirits escape?"

The old lady looked at her in amazement. "Do you think we are that ancient in our belief? No, they are open so the paint does not melt off the wood," and with a toss of the head in the normal backward motion, she was off to refill her tin cup with more costa.

Las Golondrinas

LAS GOLONDRINAS (THE SWALLOWS) WAS THE name of our new home in the Alpujarras on the southern slopes of the Sierra Nevada mountains in southern Spain. Now we just had to figure out how to get there. Returning to Somerset I got a formal written warning from my boss for taking my holiday a day early. I was so worried during my dressing down, I recorded it as a souvenir. The date we had to be back in Órgiva was August 17th. So, we could work back from there.

The house in Evercreech had to be prepared for renting, packing up would take an age, and there were resignations from all sorts of committees which needed to be addressed. School would have to be told, friends and family informed about our desertion, and direct debits cancelled. The best bit was telling my boss where to put his formal warning.

He said, "But you can't just up sticks and move to Spain, you are the best salesman we have."

Everybody's dream must be to have the opportunity to break away from the drudgery of the nine to five routine. I must say my nine to five was more like six am to ten pm. I drove over a thousand miles a week and covered most of the south of England dealing with mastitis problems and dairy hygiene solutions. The wonderful English countryside did compensate the chore somewhat. A friend who worked for a very large pharmaceutical company told me they were looking for salesmen for the autumn sales campaign. September, October and

November, and a very lucrative package for the right people, which could become an annual event.

Discussing this possibility with Sarah we decided it could be an option. My cousin Tony could drive down to Spain with Sarah, Alex, the four by four, and the caravan. I could stay back in Somerset, pack the house up properly, earn some decent money and drive down in a rented truck with all our furniture and the dog, a young springer spaniel. Sounded like a plan. I got the interview with the pharmaceutical company and I could have the job if I wanted it. We cleared the idea with Cousin Tony promising him gallons of gin for his troubles, booked the one-way ferry ticket and tried to enjoy the lovely English summer. Spanish lessons for everybody, even the dog.

With the caravan packed and the roof box on top of the car, it was time to set off for Salisbury where my cousin lived. Only three miles outside Evercreech the wheel fell off the caravan. Brilliant, what a start! Our local mechanic was soon on the case and sorted it out. Sarah drove my car and met us in Salisbury. Alex and myself knew all the words to 'Three wheels on my wagon' by the time we got there. After a tearful 'bon voyage', off they set for Portsmouth and I returned to Evercreech.

The two-night crossing from Portsmouth to Santander was a calm one, much to Sarah's relief, not being a good sailor. Alex had a whale of a time running around the ship and only getting lost once.

"Would the parents of Alexandra Bailey please report to the ship reception, she needs collecting," boomed over the tannoy.

Sarah noticed a lot of people wandering around with cameras at the ready. Whale and dolphin watchers. It was a good job none were spotted as the ship would have listed with the rush and weight suddenly transferring to one side or the other.

After a long hot journey on the road, they arrived in Orgiva safe and sound.

Getting to know Las Golondrinas and all its quirkiness was a challenge Sarah took to like a duck to water. Don't mention the water.

Tony decided to take a dip and jumped into the pool, but he jumped straight out again. The pool was officially a water store to irrigate the garden on a weekly basis. That morning the pool was emptied, cleaned and then refilled with fresh spring water pumped up from the depths of an aquifer. It was freezing cold; when you expect a pool heated by the sun and get an ice bath it's a bit of a shock. Luckily the old boy didn't have a heart attack!

Sarah drove Tony to the airport for his return to the UK, entered the car park, got Tony sorted out and went to exit. Unfortunately, there was a height barrier stopping her, the car and the roof box from leaving the car park. Having paid the parking charge she had to take the box off, which resembled a small boat, pass through the barrier and then put it back on the roof. Not one gentleman offered to help, the car park attendants just watched, and when they suggested she had to pay extra because her time had run out on the ticket, blood was nearly spilt.

Meanwhile, back at the ranch, Alex was making new friends and enjoying the constant sunshine. It was time to register for school. The lady at reception asked for her family book.

"Her what?"

Every Spanish child has a family book recording inoculation, family history etc. Sarah, on the phone, explained I needed to send all of Alex's medical records to Spain immediately.

Having a child anywhere I suppose is a bit like walking a dog in the park, you stop and chat. It's the same with kids, you meet and talk to people who have the same appendage. Alex was now being invited to tea, birthday parties, swimming parties and her friend base was now multi-cultural. That would not have happened in Somerset! Entertaining children in England is an expensive business. You save a fortune when the sun constantly shines.

It was time for school. Sarah went with Alex and spent the morning with her. In Spain they do joined up writing right from the start. Things were difficult for both of them but with persistence and enthusiasm it became easier. Six-year-olds adapt and learn. The slightly older generation just soak up the gin.

After only one week in residence Sarah noticed a lot of helicopter activity, the mountain opposite our new home and business was on fire. For four days the fire was fought by firefighters on foot and helicopters from the air. Great buckets of water swung from beneath these incredible machines flown by some very skilful and brave pilots. She described it as a scene from M.A.S.H. People's swimming pools were emptied, and it was a sense of all hands-on deck. Between us and the mountain was a river and the prevailing wind kept the destruction away from our property. But it is something to consider when looking to relocate. The danger of fire. Some friends bought in Portugal and had to make a run for it when fire engulfed their dream.

As Las Golondrinas was already a business Sarah had a steady stream of guests arriving. This was a good income stream as we had our mortgage back and that needed feeding. It also gave her some company during the evenings. When tourists are on holiday, they are very generous and require information about the area, so plenty of wine was consumed during these evening pow-wows.

Back in Somerset the new job was going well and the packing progressing. Our well-stocked freezer was being whittled down. Walking and training the puppy Maisie was great fun. To train a dog you need to be consistent and on your own. It's no good one person training it to do one thing and another confusing it with something else. We got into a routine of walking a circuit in some fields. Fetch and retrieve were going well, sit and stay and not passing the pub without some refreshment was all part of the education. Some refreshment stops went on a little longer than planned, and she would look at me as if to say, "I'm a gun dog not a guide dog."

The petrol tanker driver's strike restricted my work, but this gave me more time to organise the move. A tenant was found to rent the house. Alex's birthday was fast approaching so I flew out to be with them in Órgiva. We had a great weekend but to return to England was so difficult. I had had enough of this, a Luton van was hired, ferry tickets booked, and a date set for leaving. A friend of mine was an HGV driver and offered to help with the drive, Poole to Cherbourg. A short crossing, better for Maisie. She was not a fan of travelling in vehicles so I asked the vet if he had something that would calm her down. Ketamine tablets, a low dose of horse tranquilizer. He advised me to try it on her before as some dogs go sleepy and others get aggressive. Similar to booze on humans. I never thought I would hear of Ketamine again, but I did not know Órgiva very well then!

Off we set on November 18th, the van fully loaded. Through the port of Cherbourg, no problem, then through France, where we only got stopped once by the gendarmerie; the van was overweight, but two hundred Benson and Hedges sorted that out. Into Spain with a great cheer and heading due south for Granada. From leaving the house in Somerset to arriving in Orgiva took just twenty-five hours, incredible. Thank you, Steve. The tablets worked well for the dog. The dog's opposite from Las Golondrinas decided it was a good idea to bark all night, so they had a few sleepy tablets as well. They did sleep well and so did we!

We had a week to unload and make the return journey, but this was looking less and less attractive. To travel all that way again and then fly back to Spain.

"Steve, are you a professional driver?"

"Yes."

"Would you mind going back on your own? I might be able to find you some company."

He agreed and I was here to stay.

With Steve, the van and his travelling companion gone (with a can of air freshener - lovely girl but with hippy tendencies), it was time to fast track on our houses and gardens. Self-employed at last and in charge of our own destinies. Scary.

Las Golondrinas consisted of three casitas, on a road called La Estrella. The stars. During the clear nights with the little light pollution we had, the night sky was a festival of twinkling diamonds and the moon as bright as a powerful floodlight. The casitas were all furnished and ready to go. We decided to name the three houses on the theme of birds, as the whole place was called after a Swallow. So, we decided on, Kingfisher, Bee-eater and Hoopoe. When looking at a bird book of Spain it was a bit spooky to find all three birds next to each other in the book. The garden was not big but was so well-stocked with fruit trees it was more like a tropical greengrocer's shop. I will try to list all the trees that are producers. Here goes. Orange, Lemon, Loquat, White fig, Black fig, Kumquat, Cherimoya, Pomegranate, Avocados, Olives, Tangerines, Mandarins. Carob, Mulberry, Greengage, Plum, Cherry, JuJube, Grape, Pear, Quince, Prickly pear, Grapefruit, Clementine's, Strawberry Guava, Pineapple Guava, Tamarillo, Japanese Wine berry, Sapote, Barbados Cherry, Kiwi, Passion fruit, Walnut, Hazelnut, Almond, Clarissa (natal plums) and Cape gooseberries. During the late autumn when the Avocados are looking plump and ready to pick, we kept giving the lower ones a squeeze to see if they were ready to enjoy, but none of them were ready and ripe. Week after week we felt them and then we learnt from a Spanish friend they ripen off the tree!

The loquat (Nisbro) produces fruit similar in shape and colour to the apricot. It's the first fruit to ripen in the spring having blossomed through the winter. The new leaf appears in April resembling light green tulips pointing towards the sky ready to receive any spring rain that might come its way. It's an evergreen tree that sheds its leaves that are nearly indestructible.

The combination of good irrigation, sun and the soil, delivers the perfect conditions for cultivating almost anything. The soil structure comprises a mixture of alluvium deposits and moraine glacial flour. A very fine soil with excellent drainage but very high in nutrients and mineral content. It lacks texture but this is not a problem. Trying to add humus with the use of farmyard manure will only bring you fleas and ticks.

The garden is based on a permaculture system. "What's that?" you ask. Permaculture is a philosophy of working with nature rather than against it, it was developed in Tasmania. Seventy-eight percent of the earth's atmosphere is composed of Nitrogen gas (N2), this is not available as a nitrogenous nutrient for plants. Instead, it must be 'fixed' into ammonium (NH4) in order to use as a nutrient. Indian bean trees, southern catalpa can do this as can many other trees but in the garden of Las Golondrinas we have Indian bean trees, fixing nitrogen into the soil for the rest of the plants to benefit from. A circle of self-sufficiency.

We also have carob trees, evergreen trees that are related to the pea family, they grow fast and their limbs twist and twine with each other. Hard pruning is required to keep the trees looking in some sense of order. The carob pods can be ground down as a substitute for cocoa, and carob treat bars can be found in health food shops. I remember finding the beans in the coarse mixture we fed to calves to wean them off milk; the calves would pick them out like sweets.

Antonio, who has horses, comes and picks the pods as a supplement for their feed. The carat, a unit of mass for gemstones and of the purity of gold, takes its name from the carob seed. Spain is the third largest producer of carob, generating over 26,000 tonnes per year, just behind Portugal and Italy. The tree can sometimes be called Saint John's Bread.

Las Golondrinas was once in the river bed, you can see this by the high banks either side of us about five hundred metres apart. Our Spanish friends take the mickey, "Watch out when it rains."

The river is called the Rio Chico (Small River), but at times it is not. The irrigation is from the acequia system. On our road (camino) we are lucky to have our own spring. This runs naturally when we have sufficient rain or snow melt from higher up the mountain. When this dries up, we have a pump in the aquifer and have to purchase the water at eight euros an hour. It flows at around 35,000 litres an hour.

The Camino la Estrella is a cul-de-sac; we do not get traffic just passing through. This is a big benefit. We all have specified times to irrigate our land, when the spring has sprung, and how long we can take the water for on a weekly rota basis. There are fifty-two of us in the acequia association of the Camino la Estrella which works well. We have a wonderful acequia man called Antonio, he keeps us all in order and has to act like Henry Kissinger at times of dispute. When you put your gate in to divert the water onto your land and it's not your turn you will get a very angry neighbour wielding a mattock, ask Sarah! To some Spanish, water is more important than life. A Somerset saying, 'if water is the staff of life then cider is life itself'. Some acequias have so many members they only get water fortnightly and then God knows what time. This is all knowledge we were ignorant of when we were buying. The drinking water (agua potable) to the property was fed by a pipe so small in diameter that we all had to get holding tanks installed and a pump to provide the pressure to make the gas boiler ignite (calentador). The gas water heater is run on bottled butane and provides hot water on demand, but the bottle always seems to run out midway through a shower. This is fine if someone else is in the property but a pain in the arse when alone. Changing a gas bottle with a head full of shampoo and stinging eyes is not funny. Electric water heating is expensive, if you are lucky enough to have enough kilowatts to stop the whole house from tripping out each time the heater is switched on. The real solution is solar water heating. The systems are relatively cheap and pay back is quick, if you live here permanently. Also, we get a lot of sunshine.

As more and more properties became occupied on the camino on a full-time basis, the drinking water situation became worse and worse. In the end we were importing it from another supply. With two one-thousand litre tanks in my trailer and permission from a friend to fill them up from his tap on the other side of town, I would set off, fill the tanks and then transfer the water into our tanks using a submersible pump. But in 2012 our rough old track was dug up, a new water main installed and the road tarmacked. The inside of the old water pipe resembled a clogged lorry driver's artery. When looking for a property to buy my priority list is, access, water and then electric.

Órgiva town hall was running adult education programmes all over the Alpujarras, giving the older Spanish generation a chance to learn how to read and write. This also helped foreigners, as they were running free Spanish lessons for people like us. The local dialect is tricky to get your tongue around, they seem to swallow the words, so it's a bit like learning Geordie!

Sarah enrolled as soon as she got to Órgiva and I joined in later. On our previous holidays to France she did most of the talking as is normal. One part of the couple always tend to be more fluent than the other, so the other one lets them get on with it. The lessons were well attended (as they were free) and it was a good way to meet people who were launching on their own adventures. So, in late November I joined the classes; well, I'm not known for my dexterity on the language front. I could just not get my head around all the verbs. I have been described by some friends as being able to talk for twenty minutes in Spanish and not use one verb! The classes were held in the evenings, and after a hard day's graft often I would drop off to sleep in class. When I was awake, I could not concentrate as my mind was on building materials and foundation digging. In the end I gave up and decided to learn Spanish a different way. Bar Spanish!

The houses on the surface looked fine, a bit strange in places, but they worked. Maintenance had not been a high priority for the previous owner. They were all one bed-room properties with a kitchen, lounge and bathroom. Our aim was to make two of them into two-bedroom houses, live in one and rent the other two out.

During the coming winter I had a crash course in building an extension. On the farms I worked on we always did our own building, but fitting doors and windows was not on the list. I had a wall to build for someone else, so I calculated how many concrete blocks I needed and placed the order with the builders' merchants, six pallets of hollow blocks. The lorry turned up and the driver asked where I would like them.

"As close to the foundation of the proposed wall," I replied.

The next thing I heard was an almighty crash as the driver just tipped the whole load onto the soil. To my amazement out of 360 blocks only 6 were broken. Trying to source materials with thermal properties in the Alpujarras was difficult, so I went to Motril and found what I was after. It was near Christmas. I set off early with my car and newly acquired trailer and purchased two pallets of thermal blocks. On the counter of the builders' merchants were the traditional Christmas bottles of spirits. It was early and cold so I thought I would just have a tot of brandy. Raising my glass to the guy behind the counter he pulled out from underneath the counter nearly a pint of the stuff.

"Cheers," he said.

Obviously, an early starter. I covered the blocks up with a tarpaulin so on the way back through Órgiva I would not raise suspicion I was building and also not buying locally. A heinous crime. Permission is required from the town hall to do any type of building work even wallpapering. For small jobs you need a form from the town hall (ayuntamiento) called an obra menor.

Well these blocks were so easy to lay; I nicknamed them tonto blocks (stupid). I was back down to Motril again the next morning. No brandy this time, anise, (a liquor similar to Pernod) instead. With the walls built it was time for the roof. It's a simple block and beam flat roof in keeping with the traditional Moorish buildings. But the blocks were polystyrene which would give the room protection from the heat and the cold but also cut down on the weight of the roof. You can also get them in concrete blocks (bovedillas), or terracotta vaulted (arched) ones. Supporting the new roof with acrow props (puntales) and a layer of weld mesh on the top, it was time to lay the concrete over the whole lot. I hired a labourer for the day. As soon as we had finished it started raining, so we covered the roof with a plastic sheet to prevent some of the cement from running through to the floor below.

Andre, the labourer was soaked through, so he had a steaming hot shower and then walked up to town. I had a shower as well.

"Where's Maisie?" I asked.

She was nowhere to be found. It was still raining, December twenty-third. I went up to town and found Andre, and he said the dog had followed him up to town. Most Spanish dogs follow people around and then return home. I explained she was not a Spanish dog and what with the rain there would be no scent for her to retrace her way back. What with no Facebook to post a missing dog on, I was in despair. We had agreed to house-sit a friend's house for Christmas so we would not be at home to welcome her back. We had guests in one of the houses and they agreed to keep an eye out for her. Meanwhile, everybody we knew kept looking, but it kept on raining. Now, Orgiva being a rural town, with most of the local guys into hunting, I was sure she would be recognised as a hunting breed and taken in. When I say taken in, I mean tied up on a finca (piece of land) for most of the week and used on Sundays to hunt. That wasn't quite what I had in mind for her, also her Spanish was not so hot.

Our first Christmas in Spain will not be forgotten, the people we were house sitting for assured us there would be no guests to look after, but ten people turned up from all over the world: Sweden, the Hague, South America and France. All lovely people, but all academics. Not a practical bone in their bodies. We had to show them how to light the fires every evening. It was still raining. The Rio Gualdofeo was more like the Mississippi, a brown roaring surge snaking through the valley. My dog was still lost.

The brightest and most wonderful thing happened on Christmas Eve (Noche Bueno). We had finished work on one of the bathrooms and decided to eat out. Entering our favourite bar, Bar Canada, chatting to Angles and Nuria and explaining we were going dine, they said they were closing early as it's Christmas Eve. Everybody shuts on Christmas Eve. It's Spanish tradition.

"We all eat at home with family." Our little faces dropped, and our bottom lips started to quiver. "Why don't you come to our party for drinks?" they said. Our faces brightened, then after another conference between the girls, "Come to eat, we have plenty."

It was still raining. Having found their cortijo (farmhouse) in the back of beyond, sliding the car through the mud we entered a house full of smiles and warmth. Communication was difficult, but tolerance was there in abundance. After eating some of the largest prawns I had ever seen, a loud banging happened on the steel door, and all the Spanish kids squealed with excitement, "It's Pappa Noel," they screamed. In came a great lumbering giant with a long white beard and bright red tunic. There was a sack full of toys for everybody, the girls had even wrapped up presents for Alex. We still go to their place for Noche Bueno (good night) and it always is.

Christmas Day and still no dog, but we tried to be festive for our daughter Alex's sake. Órgiva was shut except for the bars. Christmas Day is not important to them; but it is a holiday, so life goes on as normal. No Boxing Day either. I always regarded Boxing Day as my day. Milking the cows every Christmas Day, with Boxing Day off. Hunting on horseback with the hounds or playing rugby. It was always a day that ended in misty memories. But this Boxing Day we played hunt the dog but to no avail. We knew she would not starve as oranges were her favourite and she would not die of thirst as it was still raining.

Back to the new roof. The concrete had set and had been well watered, so next came a layer of dry sand to give me the fall for the water to run off. The membrane was asphalt and needed welding together with a blow torch as it came in strips only a metre wide. Not so easy as you think, holes appeared everywhere, and every time I thought I had a good seam, another hole would appear. I had long ago given up on asphalt. When demolishing roofs, you discover how brittle it becomes, and with the extremes of temperatures we get here you need to allow for movement. This stuff just cracks. We now have a product called Ethylene Propylene Diene Monomer. EPDM. It's a rubber membrane and can be delivered to the size you require, no joints, and being rubber it is flexible. I wish I had this product a long time ago. With the roof finished, the rain stopped. Still no dog. The interior needed rendering and plastering, new skills to be learnt. The extension would give us a bedroom and a lounge. This was going to be our house.

New Year's Eve arrived, and this time last year it was the celebration to welcome the new millennium. The whole world was planning parties that would be better than other parties held in previous years. I felt we achieved quite a lot in the first year of the new millennium. New Year's Eve in Spain is celebrated in a different way than England. We went up to town around 9pm to get into the spirit of things, but it was like the Marie Celeste. We found a bar that was open. Children are allowed in bars in Spain, dogs are not.

I asked the barman, "Have we got the date wrong?"

"No, things take a while to liven up. Have you got your grapes ready?"

"What?"

At midnight, when the church bells ring in the New Year, you have to eat a grape on every chime, it brings you luck. The barman produced thirty-six grapes for us, so we stayed until 11.45pm, then, armed with our grapes and cava (Spanish bubbly) we set off for the main street. Again, it was deserted, but gradually people started appearing, and spot on twelve a throng of a couple of hundred revellers started eating their grapes. Being competitive I tucked into mine, not realising they were full of pips. I would have spent the start of the New Year in casualty if some kind soul had not practiced the Heimlich manoeuvre on me. When they say celebrate the New Year that's what they do, the Spanish party until daylight. We returned home grateful for once again having been educated in the ways of the locals.

The morning of the new year, 2001 began quite well with a phone call from a friend asking, "Have you lost a black and white dog?"

"Yes," was the reply.

"What's the dog's name?"

"Maisie."

"It's your dog."

"Where are you?"

"Las Barreras."

"I'm on my way."

When I got there it was Maisie, a little thin and her pads on her paws were worn and sore. But she was back. New Year's Day is now called Maisie Day.

Sitting down later, with Sarah, Alex and the dog, I said, "What six months we have had, I think I will start making notes, this adventure could turn into a book!"

I saw written once, 'To live a dream, plan it very carefully'. We did not have a dream, nor did we plan anything very carefully. What a gamble.

Saint Sebastian:
January 20th

PATRON OF: ARCHERS, ATHLETES, DOCTORS, HARDWARE workers, lace makers, the military, pin makers, police officers, and potters.

Sebastian was born in Gaul but grew up in Milan and died 288AD at the second attempt. He became a soldier in the army of Emperor Diocletian and achieved the rank of captain in the Praetorian guard. During his service he was a closet Christian and thus a pacifist, a sort of secret agent. On the sly he was miraculously curing gout (I could do with him here) and baptizing fellow soldiers.

As the persecution of the Christians intensified it was Sebastian who arranged for the Pope (Caius) to be hidden in a safe place. Eventually Sebastian was betrayed and sentenced to death by bow and arrow firing squad. The widow of Castulus, Irene was sent to collect his body and discovered he was not dead and nursed him back to health, only for Sebastian to confront Diocletian and dissuade him from further atrocities. On seeing the man, he thought was dead, he ordered him to be clubbed to death and thrown in the town sewer. This time dead was dead, and a woman called Lucina retrieved the body and buried it in the cemetery of Calixtus where now stands the Basilica of San Sebastian.

He became a popular art subject with Botticelli, Bernini and El Greco depicting him as a handsome youth, all but naked, tied to a stake, his body pierced with arrows with his eyes lifted in almost erotic ecstasy. Derek Jarman, the outspoken 1970's campaigner on homosexuality and the fight for gay rights even made a film about Saint Sebastian, called Sebastiane in 1976.

On a romantic Valentine's weekend in Rome (Italy v England, rugby) Sarah was quite keen to go to a catacomb, so we got the map out and made for the nearest to our hotel. Closed for renovation.

"The next one is just up the road."

Five kilometres later we were stood outside the catacomb of San Sebastian. That's a bit spooky as San Sebastian is the original patron saint of Órgiva.

San Sebastian is the patron saint of Órgiva. Cristo de la Expiracion is the patron of the Alpujarras. The Ermita of San Sebastian looks over the town and on January twentieth he is brought out of his sanctuary along with the Virgin Aurora and carried by the costaleros (trained carriers of the float, catafalque, with the Saint aboard) down to the church. A mass is then held in his honour, at 7.00pm. Then they are carried back up to the Ermita winding through the town, with the wonderful town band and priest following close behind. The solitary bell is rung up at the Ermita sounding something like a bell out of a western movie down Mexico way. The pair are then presented on their catafalques to the dark night where an elaborate firework display takes place. Quite stunning in the dark January night. Hot chocolate and churros are then offered to the faithful. This year they brought them back down again to the church and more fireworks were set off.

Agriculture and Mining

THE DEFINITION OF AGRICULTURE IS: THE art or science of cultivating the ground. I suppose having a background in farming this would naturally draw oneself to a rural area, the same as if you were from a coastal area to the sea. Órgiva is definitely a rural town. Not quite what I had been used to, but there is a bond of kinship when farming is discussed. No green rolling hills with cows and sheep grazing peacefully on their own. No hum of milking machines early in the mornings. Milking goats is a once a day job and normally carried out at a sociable hour, mid-morning. Different sounds and routines, but definitely production from the land. In an arid part of the world where water is at a premium, but space is ample, the farmer has to adapt.

My passion for farming started as a child. My Uncle Reg had a wonderful farm in Devon right on the border of Cornwall just outside Launceston, my home town. Reg was married to my dad's sister, Betty. They were staunch Methodists, chapel twice on a Sunday, no swearing, no drinking, but farming was their thing. Efficient, go-ahead, organised. I loved spending time at Polson Farm.

I remember as early as the age of six helping out at lambing time. My uncle would cut the sleeves off an old raincoat and put them over my legs to act as leggings to keep the rain and mud off my trousers, held up by bailer twine onto my belt which was also bailer twine.

Once we were bringing in a newly born set of triplets, I was carrying the smallest (just), when the maternal mother (Devon long wool) butted me square in the back sending me flying into the mud face down. My uncle told me when I was older, that when I stood up, all he could see were my eyes, the rest of me was just mud. Him and my cousin, Graham had to try really hard to contain their amusement. I picked up the lamb and carried on walking to the loose box making the bleating noise so the mother would follow. He said most six-year-olds would have burst into tears or never gone near a sheep again.

Small hands were very useful when a ewe (female sheep) was in trouble giving birth, the lamb having a leg back, or two lambs coming at once, a jumble of legs not knowing which legs belonged to which lamb. Or even breech (backwards).

Every weekend or school holiday I would spend on the farm, getting older and stronger and more useful, milking, hay making, and harvesting the grass to make silage for the dairy herd. This was a traditional mixed farm. Not much was bought in, barley was grown to be milled and fed to the stock, and the straw was used as bedding for the winter when the cattle were housed.

The mill house was close to the farmhouse. Upstairs was level with the field above so the raw materials could be delivered by tractor. The mill and mix produced the concentrate for the dairy herd, young stock, beef cattle and the sheep. This would come down to the ground floor in hoppers ready to be bagged off into hessian sacks, fifty kilograms a piece. At the age of twelve I could fill the sacks and drag them away but not lift them. It was during this work I had an accident that would affect and alter my life for ever. I fell off a vertical loft ladder landing on my right buttock from three metres high. Apart from a dark and angry looking bruise everything seemed fine. It was eleven years later I discovered that the fall had damaged the femoral neck and head, arthritis had attacked my femoral head and it resembled the shape of a fifty pence coin, a heptagon. I wondered why it was so painful. A total hip replacement was needed but at twenty-three I was too young. I had to wait.

Well, my vocation was set in stone (not being aware of my hip damage, if so, I would have taken up knitting). Agriculture it was to be. I studied hard, I had to, learning and education were always a struggle for me, my head would be on the sports field or on the farm, but with the right incentive and a target to aim for I got my exams and went to Sparsholt Agricultural College, near Winchester. It took me years to realise I was lucky to have the choice, envious of the farmers' sons and daughters that had their future handed to them on a plate. They had no choice, but I did.

I was on a three-year course, OND General Agriculture. A sandwich course, one year in, one year out and the final year in. During my middle year I obtained the top placement, working for the Queen's uncle, Lord Mountbatten of Burma on his estate, Broadlands at Romsey. I graduated with a credit.

The main livestock farming in and around Órgiva are goats and sheep. Many years ago, enough rain fell in the area to farm cows for milk. Lactating cows have a far greater appetite than those bred for beef, so when the climate changed the farming changed. A lactating cow would consume a lot of preserved forage over a six-month winter, if you can't grow it you can't preserve it. Goats on the other hand can graze and forage all year round.

I would like to give you a crash course on dairy cow management.

A dairy cow will have her first calf at the age of two after a gestation period of 283 days, this will trigger her lactation. This lactation and the ones in front of her will last 305 days, she will then be dry for 60 days, a holiday, before she has another calf, completing a calving index of 365 days.

If you have a herd of dairy cows your aim is to achieve a calving index of 365 days. This means you have a well-run herd with good fertility and maximising profitability. Other factors will get in the way, mastitis, lameness and age. With the milk price better in the winter, it was fashionable to calve as many cows as possible in the autumn. When the cows are housed for the winter you have more control of their diets. To feed a dairy efficiently it is best to feed her on what you can grow yourself on the farm. Grass and maize are the bulkiest food. A cow housed for the winter will consume ten tonnes of preserved forage. Let's take a 600kg black and white cow. At the peak of her lactation, around eight weeks from calving, she could be producing 50 to 60 litres of milk a day, convert that to pints. One hundred pints of milk on your doorstep every day. That's a lot of milk, from one cow. To feed this cow accordingly, she needs forage, from this forage she needs protein and energy. The forage will not provide enough, so a concentrated food needs to be introduced. To produce 1 litre of milk a cow needs five megajoules of energy, multiply this by 50, 250 megajoules of energy. Plus, more energy to maintain her body and more energy to ovulate and become pregnant again. Plus, the protein.

A cow's ration is based on how much dry matter she can consume. (Dry Matter Intake.)

A 600kg cow can consume 5% of her body weight in dry matter per day, that equates to 30 kg of dry matter or 107kg of fresh food per day at 28% dry matter content of her ration.

So, a proportion of the diet has to be in a concentrated form to give her all that energy and protein.

When I started milking cows the concentrate was measured in percent of protein, that was the terminology we used. A 16% concentrate was common. The protein derived from soya or wheat. As pressure mounted on production and more milk had to be produced from home grown forage, a higher protein concentrate was demanded by the farmer and his nutritionist.

An 18% concentrate was produced using white fish meal as the source of the protein.

Next was the problem of getting enough of this protein into the cow. They would be milked twice a day so during milking they were fed the concentrate. Cows like concentrate, like sweets to a child. But this was like presenting the richest chocolate brownie you have ever seen. Eat half of that now, and half later. Impossible without feeling sick. What if we could slice up the brownie and give it to her in portions, she would then eat up the whole thing without being ill?

Introducing out of parlour feeders. Brilliant, a necklace was placed around the cow with her number printed on it and a transponder that would talk to a computer. When she entered the feeder a portion of concentrate would drop down in front of her. Eight to ten times a day. The computer would tell me if she did not eat up her ration and so became a very useful stockman ship aid as well. The farmer now seeing the potential of upping the protein portion of the diet even further pressurized the feed producing companies to produce a 22% protein concentrate. How? Bone and meat. Feeding their own bodies back to the herbivores. Mechanically Recovered Meat. This in my opinion is how mad cow disease started. The chemical and medical proof in another subject. Greed, and pressure on profit.

Sheep have had a brain disease for centuries called scrapie. The symptoms are the same as mad cow disease.

There were a few reported cases of BSE in northern Spain, but not many in France as the French farmer knew the consequences. In France it was called JCB disease. If they had a suspected infection, they would dig a hole, kill the beast and bury it. Hence JCB.

Farming goats for milk is an extensive form of farming, no pressure on investment, no quotas to reach, milking once a day. The larger goat farmers have modern milking systems with bulk tanks to store the milk in and keep it cool, but you still see a van full of milk churns waiting for the milk tanker to arrive to suck the milk out. Milk churns were banned in the UK in 1979, a so-called European directive. The local goat farmers take the animals out to graze normally after lunch. Free grazing, up and down the barranco, grazing land that has not been fenced, so farming without owning land is possible. Just like England before the Enclosures Act in 18th century. Common land that enabled peasants to farm for their subsistence. Next time you consider erecting a fence around your piece of Spain think about the effect on the local campesino and his few goats.

A female goat is called a doe, a male a billy. Does normally have their first kid at a year and a half, or when they reach 35kg in weight. They have a gestation period of 150 days; they are poly oestrus which means they only breed or cycle during the shorter days of the year. They produce about 2.5kg of milk a day. The butter fat content is 3.5%. Goat milk produces 2% of milk produced worldwide. Goats' milk has small, well emulsified fat globules which means the cream remains suspended in the milk instead of rising to the top. This means it is great for making into cheese. The milk tanker in the Órgiva area picks the refrigerated milk up every four days, testing for cleanliness, quality and making sure no water has accidently been added.

A friend had a few goats and one of them was due to give birth. I got a phone call, the doe, giving birth for the first time, was really struggling and needed assistance, could I come over and help? So off I went in a bit of a hurry, and the local police pulled me over and asked why I was speeding. I explained in my poor Spanish, I had a goat waiting for me! They said slow down and wear protection!

The doe was straining like mad and in quite a state. I managed to push the kid back in and correct a leg that was back, as they should be born in a position like a diver entering a pool. The kid was born and was quite small.

"I reckon there is another one on its way," I said and there was. Triplets. All okay. I then looked up the word for midwife in Spanish (comadrona).

Because of the roaming grazing nature of the animals, worm control is impossible by rotation. A normal life cycle of a roundworm, tapeworm is eighteen to twenty-one days, so if no goats graze that land for this length of time then the life cycle will be broken, but as soon as one herd of goats has grazed another one soon follows, so worm control has to be done using medicines. Ectoparasites are the external problems like mange, ticks and fleas, Endoparasites are the internal ones.

It was my first birthday here in Spain and we decided to have a goat curry to celebrate. I asked our local goatherd if I could buy a goat for eating and he said he would bring one over. Antonio appeared in his car, opened up the boot and there were two goats alive.

"Which one do you want?" he asked.

"What's best?" I replied.

"This one."

So, off we went to dispatch the creature. When in the woods Antonio offered me the knife to do the deed. No problem. The look on his face was one of amazement. I explained my farming history. I think the story circulated quite quickly as I started to get lots of 'holas' from the locals.

Choto, is how most goat is eaten in the campo, it's normally the guys who organise the fiesta and do the cooking. Women can't cook goat!

This is how it goes. Obtain two dead cleaned goats, around the 15kg mark. Smash the whole lot up using an axe but leave the heads intact. Light the fire in the Cortijo, grind up loads of dried red peppers, twenty bulbs of garlic, bay leaves, oregano, marjoram, stale bread and lashings of white wine. Chuck the whole lot in the massive pan, cook until the meat is tender and drink lots of costa. Place the pan onto the table, no plates, a plastic fork for everybody, lots of bread and tuck in, and spit all the splintered bone out as you go. There might be a crude salad in a washing up bowl as well. Afterwards, all the rubbish into a bin bag, wash up the pan, get the cards and the whiskey out and play Rentoy. If you are lucky you might get coffee. Keep it simple. It took me three of these events to learn how to pace myself and I still don't understand Rentoy!

Mules are still used for hauling materials up to inaccessible areas, some carrying up to 90kg dead weight, 20% of its body weight. A horse could carry a rider up to 30% of its body weight but that's live weight. A mule is a cross between a male donkey and a female horse, the other way around and it is called a Hinny. A mule is sterile (99% percent of the time). They were used extensively by the military for hauling cannons into positions of strategic importance. The mule has the ground covering ability of the dam, but the strength of the sire, they consume less food and are more independent than their equine cousins.

The most common breed of sheep in the area are Segurena, gangly looking things that are suited to the climate and the terrain. In the UK we have more different breeds of sheep than any other country. Sixty-three to be precise and then lots of crossbreeds as well. All bred and developed for the different areas of the UK.

Segurenas are scavengers of anything green, they are not fenced in neat fields with lush grazing but are constantly on the move, searching for forage, and the shepherd (pastor) will be with them all the time, like the goatherd. In the UK we have some fantastic grasses all developed by various plant breeding stations all over the country. Some of the varieties are like rocket fuel and others are developed for long term permanent pastures. This is impossible to do in southern Spain as the summers are too hot to sustain the plants. Lucerne is drought resistant and can survive arid conditions but not very common in our area. A good leg of lamb in England will feed a family of four, a leg of Segurena lamb will feed one.

The larger flocks of sheep will move up the mountain as the summer progresses, chasing the grazing. The shepherd will base himself up there for a few months at a time. Quite a lonely existence but made easier by today's mobile phones. It's quite funny to think a shepherd could be a couple of thousand metres above sea level checking his Facebook or watching a streamed movie.

The history of sheep and their shepherds goes back centuries in Spain and one of the oldest unions was created due to sheep. On a trip to Segovia I learnt of a group of sheep farmers who had set up a union in the 13th century called the Honrado Concejo de la Mesta, Honourable Council of the Mesta. They grazed the strip of land called no-man's land, a 100km wide track between the Christians and the Moors, which was too dangerous for arable production. The Mesta became the most powerful agriculture union ever. They set up the drovers' trails so the flocks of sheep could be moved with the seasons. These trails still exist today and are called Cañadas, or Cañadas Real (royal trail). Some of them go through the middle of Madrid and at times are still used and seeing a flock (rebano) of 5,000 sheep herded through the city is quite amusing.

A well-known local author called me up and asked if I could help Ali dispatch a few lambs. Ali is a Bangladeshi builder who also knew the Halal method of slaughter. "No problem," I said. It was a long drive to the farm but once we got there it must have been a strange sight, Ali dressed in his white robes and carrying a samsonite case with the tools of his trade and me limping on beside him up the dusty track.

Sheep need to be shorn of their fleece once a year, it's a legal requirement in the UK. The wool price fluctuates a great deal and a few years ago the price was so bad it cost more to get the sheep shorn than the wool was worth. Now wool is back in fashion it has again become economical to shear. In the UK we get a lot of Antipodeans come over for the shearing season. Here, there is a guy in Órgiva who organises the shearing of thousands of sheep across Andalucía. South Americans fly over and do the shearing, earning a good wage to take back home. The battered old transit vans return to Órgiva with the shearing boards attached to the roofs. It's quite amusing seeing the shearers wander around Órgiva at the end of the season, early July, tanned like wrinkly old walnuts, lining up in the bank to receive their wedge of cash. In excess of one million sheep are shorn per year by this team, at one euro seventy cents that's a good income. They all purchase shoes for some reason to take back to Peru, Argentina and Paraguay. It's amazing what you can observe in this fascinating town.

We decided to keep some chickens, so I built a chicken arch with wheels so we could move it around. As I was building the thing a few neighbours took an interest.

"Chickens, you will need a cockerel then."

"What for?"

"You won't get any eggs without a cockerel."

I looked after 60,000 battery hens, we had an egg a day from each of them and not a cockerel in sight.

I know battery farming is cruel, but to have enough free-range eggs for England alone you would need an area the size of Dorset to accommodate them. The people of Dorset would not be happy with that would they?

With the amount of pigs' legs hanging about you would expect to find a few pigs in Andalucía. On the contrary, they are all imported from the wheat, barley and acorn growing areas of Spain. The pigs are farmed where their food source is and then slaughtered and the legs and shoulders brought to the Alpujarras for curing and drying. It's big business. The high mountain villages look well populated by the amount of buildings you can see, but don't be fooled, most of the buildings are for the legs and shoulders of the famous jamon to dry in.

I was in Trevelez one morning, which is the most famous of all the jamon villages, being the highest above sea level, and it was 10am, breakfast time for workers. Suddenly men were appearing out of the secaderos (jamon factories) dressed in their white overalls scurrying off like ghosts for their coffee and precious bocadillos.

Embutedas are the other products made from the pig, salami, peperoni, air dried fillet of pork, sausages, a spread called sobrasada and other delicacies, all squeezed into skins for the fermentation process (the manganese in pepper helps the fermentation process) and the preservation. The Spanish call plump ladies who wear tight dresses, embutidas! Mutton dressed as lamb.

The most common breed of pig used is the Landrace, but also the Iberian black (the acorn eaters). The process is quite simple, once the joints are delivered, they are cleaned and trimmed. Then they are covered in sea salt for a couple of weeks, washed and hung in the secaderos to let the mountain air do its thing. They can be left curing for up to eighteen months. In supermarkets and bars, you can see the legs hanging up with an upside-down mushroom stuck in the lowest part of the joint. This is to catch any fat that drips off.

The labyrinth of the acequia system feeds the whole area with water for irrigation. Each parcel of land be it high in the mountains, down in the fertile valleys, in the middle of towns or in remote villages, all have their quota of water written into the title deeds of the real estate. The Romans recognised the abundant water supply from the snow melt and set about building a system to harness this precious resource. The Moors refined the distribution. Acequias can be witnessed all over the world, from Mexico to the southern states of North America. In Morocco, on a trip to the Atlas Mountains, we came across Moorish acequia channels. The common denominator seems to be the snow-covered mountains that provide the slow continuous supply of water. If the precipitation was all rain and not snow, then storing a sudden downpour would be difficult to collect unless a modern-day dam has been constructed. Snow has its uses.

Very large holding tanks (alburcas) are constructed high in the mountains to collect the water and supply the life blood during the dry months. This is controlled by a team of acequia men who from knowledge passed down from father to son know the water channels like the back of their hand. Some of these channels are on such a slow gradient the water appears not to be moving or even displaying that optical illusion of travelling uphill. These acequias need constant care and maintenance so all who receive the water contribute through different associations to their upkeep. During dry years water can be pumped up from deep underground aquifers and again entitlement to this supply is recorded in the title deeds. Be wary during wet years of cheap property being sold with its own spring, in dry years which outnumber wet ones your newly acquired oasis can be as arid as a pub with no beer!

The form of irrigation is normally flood irrigation, this is a very wasteful method, but most run off returns to the acequia channel to be used by someone else down the line. Cultivation is by rotovating the soil by machines that have scoop shape blades set to a particular depth. This causes a problem in itself as a pan or crust is formed below the surface and any irrigation water that soaks into the soil will only penetrate to the pan thus not getting to the all-important root systems of the plants and trees. Sub-soiling is required to break the pan. Drip feeding water is a much more economical way of irrigating but with the high temperatures during the summer months constant checks are needed as green algae can block the black pipe feeders. The Spanish Government has decreed that by 2020 all irrigation should be by drip feeding. There will be revolutions in the Alpujarras.

Organic status is gaining in popularity and takes a long time to qualify for the right to be classed organic. Some visiting organic farmers from Australia told us that to be organic in Australia you need your own water source. My question is, how can a farm in the Alpujarras be organic when the water you use to irrigate with has travelled over so many other people's land that might be using all sorts of nasty fertilizers, pesticides and herbicides?

When watering your land just remember that the bottom terrace wall of your land is yours. It is always like this. Why? If you over water and the wall or bank subsides on to your neighbour's land you have to rebuild it. Irrigate with care.

The acequia channels have claimed many victims. An English saying is 'one for the road', well in Órgiva it's 'una para la acequia'.

Sarah had an accident in the acequia, coming home one evening she noticed water flowing past our land and decided to place our gate into the slot and water our land. On bending down to position the metal gate in place she over balanced and fell into the gulley, her sandals disappeared downstream and a rather nasty gash on her head was gushing with blood. By the time the rest of us returned home the house resembled a murder scene. There was blood everywhere, and the shower looked like a slaughter house killing room. Tiptoeing through to the bedroom, there she was, fast asleep as if nothing had happened.

Cars often end up stuck in the acequia. One guy got both a front and back wheel in and had to be lifted out with a crane. On another event a drunk got so wedged in it took three strong blokes to lift him out. If the water had been flowing, he would have taken his last drink.

One of our cats is not stupid, during the hot summer months you can often find her asleep beside the concrete pipe where the irrigation water comes in, as the cool draught caused by the water rushing by outside acts like an air conditioner. The acequia also has another use. On visiting a property for sale on behalf of a friend, I enquired why no toilet should be flushed down the loo.

"Are the pipes too small to take the paper?" I asked.

"No," replied the owner, "we don't like to see the paper in the acequia." The sewage goes directly into the irrigation water. Lovely. Don't fill your pool up with that water.

The land in and around Órgiva produces an array of crops, Olives being the main income, but Avocados are being planted in their thousands, the height above sea level is marginal but they seem to survive and thrive. A couple of hectares can produce five to six tonnes a year bringing in a good income. they are easy to harvest but do like ample water. On the coast mangos are in fashion, replacing cherimoya as a cash crop. Oranges and lemons light up the fincas during the winter months, but as an income-producing crop they do not figure very high, unless you harvest them and sell them on the road side to passing tourists. Citrus trees have a life of fifty years or so, and they need feeding and pruning. Pollenization is an important aspect of fruit production and lately this has not been as normal as it should be. Ask yourself how many insects are hitting your windscreen, not so many as before?

The inheritance system has reduced the size of farms to an extent that sustainable parcels of land have been so carved up they become hobby allotment gardens. A shed is built to store the tools and crops in, then northern Europeans turn up and buy these plots for a king's ransom, turn the allotment shed into a house and live the dream.

You don't realise the number of almond trees there are until they are in blossom, and from January through to March these trees show off a display of truly amazing colours. These rapidly turn into small furry fruits that fill out and by the end of August they are ready to harvest. Incredible trees surviving sometimes just on the morning dew. With nets and a good stick, you bring the fruits to the floor to be cleaned of the husk. One year an ice storm at the end of August, beat me to it and I had to pick all the fruits off the ground as I had no chance to put the nets down. Almond trees are frequently grafted to improve the fruits' sweetness. You need a lot of trees to make any money but again for your own consumption you can't beat it. Garlic and almond soup served cold with some grapes on the top (ajo blanco). I never quite understood the rhyme, gathering nuts in May! The almond is a fruit related to the peach.

The pomegranate has a long history in the area, as the fruit in Spain is known as the Grenadina, which translates into Granada or New Granada if you are in Columbia. The fruit is the symbol of Granada and is depicted all over the city in various obscure places. The tree blossoms late May, early June with crimson trumpet flowers that rapidly turn to small fruit by the start of July with a crown on the fruit resembling the orb from the film Frozen. The fruit is ready by early spring and the juice has magical properties. The seeds or arlis contain the juice. It is said to be beneficial in skin and hair condition, anti-ageing, heart disease, anaemia, Alzheimer's, improves digestion, reduces blood pressure, strengthens bones and even prevents cancer. The juice contains, protein, dietary fibre, minerals such as potassium, magnesium, iron, calcium, phosphorous, zinc and sodium, anti-oxidants, vitamins K, C, E, Folate, Thiamine, Riboflavin, Niacin and no cholesterol, but high in calories due to the sugar content. The fruit can be stored whole for many months. Get hold of some stockings or tights (old ones, not the wife's latest purchase), pick the heaviest non-damaged globes, fill up the hosiery and hang them in a cool, dry, dark place. I say heaviest as they will have more juice in them. The husk of the fruit is full of benefits as well. Sun dry it and grind it up, it is great against acne, ageing, and dandruff, and is used as a moisturiser, facial scrub, and sunscreen. ix it with hot water and sieve, drink for sore throats, heart strength, dental health and gut health. I have seen dogs tucking into the dried husk, it contains an Anathematic which produces an Alkaloid, this is poisonous to tape worms and other endoparasitic infestations.

The prickly pear (chumba) is a great digester of sewage, you normally would see this growing in or around the waste pipe of the farmhouse. It also acts as a good fire break. We have septic tanks these days to catch the waste. If you are tempted to pick a prickly pear be warned, they have thousands of tiny thorns that will cause you discomfort for a very long time, because they are so small you can't see the little blighters to pull them out, so wear a glove. They do taste nice but only consume two at the maximum, as they have greater constipation properties than eggs.

The cactus seems invincible but an infection from the cochineal insect has caused widespread devastation of the hardy plant. The history of this insect is so important to Spain it's worth investigating. In the 16th century Hernan Cortes and his conquistadors arrived in Mexico. Stunned by the vibrant colours that surrounded them, they noticed the red colour in particular was intense. The colour red in Europe was an emblem of power and wealth. The Turks produced a red dye by using cow dung, rancid olive oil and oxen blood, dull and but not very pleasant.

How did the Aztecs produce this dye? By the female cochineal insect. Harvested from Opuntia cactus, the insect was then dried and the carminic acid inside the insect produced the colour. Nineteen to twenty-two percent of its body weight contains the pigment. Cortes was so excited by this discovery he wrote to the king of Spain describing its potential. By 1560 25kg of the dye had been imported and by 1585 100kg. The value, weight for weight was worth more than gold. And printer ink! This made Spain rich and touched most of Europe by producing rich red dyes for garments and robes. Tanners also used it, and artists clambered to use it in their work, The

Incredulity of Saint Thomas by Caravaggio shows how vibrant cochineal made the work compared to older versions. Rubens' portrait of Isabella Brandt (1610) highlights the glow that this dye introduced to art work. But by the mid-19th century a synthetic substitute took over. So those annoying little white flies (the male cochineal) that get through the fly screens and cover everything are responsible for quite a piece of Spanish history.

We seem to have a perpetual blossom season from the loquat and medlar in the autumn to the crimson red of the pomegranate in June, giving the bees lots of work to do. The delicate pinks of the membreo (quince) to the white of the pear. Broad beans planted in October are in flower in January along with yellow oxalis and a carpet of violets. I have seen a local with a bag of wild asparagus in February picked from a secret spot. In sheltered areas we even get bananas, sweet orange coloured ones; bananas are classified as an herb. The fig tree is very common and can fruit twice a year. The first fruit are called Brevas. The fruit form early before the leaves are on the tree, and they ripen towards the end of June, are bigger, less sweet and purple. The second, Higos, are ready in the autumn, are green and sweet. Figs are so wonderful straight off the tree but also dry very well, which makes it easier for transportation.

It's strange to witness sheep and goats grazing tarmac, but when the ripe fig falls to the ground onto the tarmac the animals go crazy for them. Just a warning, the sap of the fig burns the skin and the wood gives off noxious gasses if burnt in a confined space.

Grapes are found everywhere, creating rapid shade and some great by-products. The wine made locally is called costa and can be rose to light brown in colour, but don't let that fool you. Some guests once bought a litre to drink back at the casita; we didn't see them the next day! They call it organic; I call it lethal. Up on the Contraviesa, the mountains between Órgiva and the sea, there is a bodega called Four Winds (cuatro vientos). Now this a proper wine making setup. Its bodega is well worth a visit and they are producing some fantastic wines with new varieties introduced to the area. Grape harvesting time in Spain is called the Vendimia. Back breaking work as most vines are called vines of the earth and grow along the ground not strung up on wires for ease of harvest.

Late September the foliage of the summer's plants begins to die and wither revealing the stunning blood reds, scarlets, and crimsons of the peppers and tomatoes, ready for eating or preserving for the coming winter. The local diet really does follow the seasons. Autumn rain, the clouds sit like pockets of candy floss in the mountain valleys and gullies. I remember some guests arriving during the night and not realising the mountainous terrain that surrounded them. When they arose the next day, the whole area was shrouded in mist and then like a shy mistress revealed herself to them. Their astonishment was tangible.

The rich soil in the valley of Tijola produces a mountain of vegetables, cropping three times a year. It's great to know the vegetables sold every Thursday in the wonderful Órgiva market are produced locally. Farther up in the mountains you come across seas of ripening tomatoes, cherries dripping off the trees, fields of French beans, apples and of course chestnuts.

Mulberries are grown mainly in gardens now for the fruit, it's great to see children gorge themselves on the berries, covered in the juice and looking like they have been in a blood bath. The mulberry played an important role in the history of the Alpujarras. The silk industry.

The silk worm (bombyx mori) was discovered over five thousand years ago in China. Allegedly a silk cocoon dropped off a tree into a hot cup of tea and seeing how the fine thread unravelled itself from the chrysalis it was investigated further, and silk was discovered. This sounds plausible, but it makes you wonder how olive oil was discovered. Take an olive off the tree and chew it, you will soon spit it out, tested on humans not on animals!

The silk worm is born tiny and covered in black hairs but in four weeks it has increased its body weight by 10,000 times and is now 7.5cm long, white and fat. The cocoon starts to develop and in two weeks the moth will leave to lay another 300 eggs. The silk worm is attracted to the mulberry leaf by a chemical fragrance Cis-Jasmone. The first new leaves of the season burst from the tree in late April, early May. One cocoon can produce 1,000 metres of single thread, but you will need between 2,000 and 3,000 cocoons to produce half a kilo of silk.

At one time in the 13th century there were five hundred villages in the Alpujarras growing Mulberry trees on the terraces watered from snow melt to feed the silk worms that produce the silk thread for the four thousand looms to produce the valuable fabric. The mountain terraces of the Alpujarras looked more like the tea field of Assam with the flowing green foliage waving in the breeze from May until October. The raw silk was taken to the Alcaiceria souk in Granada, processed, taxed and sold. Granada silk was a high-quality product in great demand. The Moor king Boabdil had his cloaks made from this local yarn. One of his famous quotes referred to the area, "I would rather have a grave in Granada than a house in the Alpujarras". There are examples of Granada silk all over the world, in Valencia in the Lonja Silk Exchange, Copenhagen, London, and Paris. The material Percale (Perxal) was mentioned in 1384 in Valencia and was believed to contain a certain amount of silk. The Acaiceria souk can still be found in Granada next to the cathedral, it used to be much larger but a fire in 1800 destroyed a lot of the labyrinth of alleyways. The Alpujarras were known Europe wide as the Country of Silk. An outbreak of Pebrina in the 15th century wiped out the silk worm population and also the silk trade with it. Quite often Alex our daughter would come home from school with a jam jar containing silk worms and Mulberry leaves, and her parents were quite ignorant about the importance of these worms to the history of the area and of Granada.

A Mulberry tree even exists in Wakefield prison, in the exercise yard. This is where the song "here we go around the Mulberry bush" allegedly originates from, as the female inmates would sing it as they exercised in the moonlight. A cloth is produced from the bark of the Mulberry tree, called Tapa. It is very popular in the South Sea islands and is used in ceremonial garments worn by local chiefs, very cool.

There is a more modern-day cash crop grown in the Alpujarras these days. Marijuana. On rooftop terraces, under the canopy of chestnut trees, in redundant roofed swimming pools or just out in the open. In mid-September a trailer loaded to the gunnels with Marijuana plants could be towed up the high street in Órgiva, this gets the noses twitching, another haul for the Guardia Civil. It's strange they wait to confiscate it just before it is ready for harvesting!

The authorities tend to turn a blind eye to a plant grown for your own enjoyment but when that becomes a plantation, they come down hard.

Benificio is a hippy commune, above Órgiva, the land bought by Welsh tipi dwellers from the valley of Llandeilo, Carmarthenshire over thirty years ago. The Welsh winters got too harsh for some so they would migrate south for warmth and favourable growing conditions. Israel's so-called conscientious objectors running away from conscription found they could hide there, above Órgiva but got in trouble by stealing other people's irrigation water and not for growing the plant.

Tobacco is grown by the locals and enjoyed by many old timers, again in small quantities with the authorities not interfering. During the civil war Franco controlled the Canary Islands early in the conflict which meant he controlled the tobacco industry. A powerful weapon for the fighters on the front. To this day the (Estancos) Tobacconists are controlled by the government and franchises handed out to families that supported the cause.

We live in an area full of amazing palm trees, adorning many a well-planned out garden. In 1994 the first sign of the destructive Red Palm Weevil reared its ugly head in Spain. It took another fifteen years before it started killing palm trees up here in the Alpujarras. The weevil attacks nineteen different spices of palm, but the one they seemed to enjoy the most was the Phoenix Canariensis. Palm trees with great spreading fronds suddenly went limp, as they were being destroyed by the weevil burrowing up to a metre into the trunk of the tree. If you put your ear to the plant you could hear the larva gorging themselves.

Disposing of dead palm trees is not easy, the dead fronds can be burnt, but the trunks stand like rotten teeth scarring the landscape. You might have seen on television hurricanes battering tropical islands, but the palm trees just bend with the wind. They are so full of fibre they don't snap and break. Imagine tackling a dead palm tree with a chainsaw, the chain and the bar just gets clogged up with matted fibre. They are also too wet to burn, so you can't pull them out. A JCB is normally the solution but access is difficult especially across someone's beloved garden. Prevention is the best solution using a systemic insecticide and regular treatment costing a small fortune. An Italian firm invented a microwave collar to zap the trees killing the weevils. When a seaside town has a promenade full of palms, they will go to any lengths to protect and preserve the essence of their seafront.

Production is not just off the land in this part of the Alpujarras it's underneath it as well. Mining.

It is thought the Greeks started to explore the rocks around Órgiva. There is a village in the Contreviesa called Polopus, which sounds Greek to me! Then the Carthaginians. But it was the Romans who explored the deepest and found iron deposits. Another village in Sierra Nevada is called Ferilloa. Ferrous meaning iron. The name of an ironmonger's in Spanish is a Ferreteria. The first real documented potential of the Sierra de Lujar came at the end of the 18th century. In 1795 the priest in Órgiva, Gabriel de Ledesma described the mountain as having all kinds of mineral deposits. In 1856 concessions were granted and lead and copper were extracted from over 60 pits. A company was formed known as the Minas y Polomos de Sierra de Lujar. During the great depression of the 1920's the company became worthless. A Belgian engineer, Louis De Pelsmaeker bought the mines and made them flourish in spite of limited resources. He married a local girl from Órgiva and cared about the lives of the miners and their families. In 1944 he sold his mines to a French company. S A Penaroya. A total of 300 men were now employed, with the village of Tablones being the processing site for the ore. Lead provided good profits for the company, but in 1970 large deposits of fluorite were discovered. This was a mineral in demand and by 1983 18,000 tonnes were sold. Cheaper imported fluorite from Mexico and Morocco put pressure on the mines and in 1989 the mines closed. More than 2,500,000 tonnes of spoil were extracted from the mountains leaving behind 140km of tunnels.

In 2016 the workings were reopened, and the quality of the fluorite examined. The quality was of some of the best in Europe, so the mines are back in business employing some 80 men working round the clock in eight-hour shifts.

Fluorite is a mineral also sometimes called fluorspar and acid spar, $CaF2$, it is categorised by its level $CaF2$. Metallurgical 60-85%, Ceramic 85-96% and Acid 97%+. A tonne is worth 380 euros, but this is expected to rise to 440 euros by 2020. Its main use is as a flux in the smelting industry, also in certain glass and enamel applications. The best grade of fluorite is used to manufacture Hydrofluoric Acid, creating lenses with a low dispersion ideal in the production of telescopes and microscopes. The mineral itself comes in many different colours and is used in healing; it's known as the Rainbow Keeper. Also recognised as your spiritual vacuum cleaner for the dust in your head, very suitable for this dusty paradise!

Mining is not normally a chosen profession for the men at the coal face, so to speak. To study mining is a vocation, to work as a miner is of necessity. It's local employment. No one would choose to do that sort of work, with the dangers to health through accidents or breathing in nasty carcinogens. But work is work and history shows of generations of mine workers being miners because they were born in the wrong place. There is a specialist college in Cornwall called the

Camborne School of Mines. They say if there is a mine anywhere in the world you will find a Cornishman down it. Why is there a pasty fiesta in Pachuca, Mexico? Mining, Cornwall has produced some of the best hard mineral miners and engineers in the world. As an optimist, and with most of the coal mines now shut in northern England, at least the indigenous population there now have a choice of occupation.

Saint Mark / San Marcos
April 25th
Evangelist

PATRON OF CATTLE BREEDERS, LANTERN MAKERS, notaries, Egypt and Venice.

Mark the evangelist was also known as John Mark. Mark was the cousin of Barnabas. Being an evangelist means he wrote one of the four gospels. It also means a person who proclaims good news. Matthew, Luke and John are the other three evangelists.

He was the author of the second gospel and is symbolized by a winged lion. Mark became the first bishop of Alexandria and was martyred there. He was dragged through the streets with a rope around his neck and then strangled. I would have thought the dragging would have been sufficient. It is believed that Mark was on board a ship sheltering from a storm in a lagoon now called San Francesco della Vigna, which is where Venice is built. An angel appeared and promised a great city would be built there in his honour. Mark's relics were stuck in Alexandria until 829 when merchants of Venice smuggled them out covered in pork which the superstitious Moors would not touch. His relics now rest beneath the high altar of the Cathedral of San Marco, Florence.

Tablones and Carataunas, two villages close to Órgiva, celebrate San Marcos. Tablones is across the River Gualdafeo to the south and Carataunas is eight hundred metres above sea level overlooking Órgiva to the north. Each fiesta is different. Tablones is a well-populated village and they know how to party. A lot of people that live in Órgiva have connections with Tablones. The fiesta is moved to the nearest weekend. A marquee is erected in the plaza next to the church with a stage. Tablones rock takes place on Friday night with local punk, rock, and heavy metal bands belting out their stuff until the early hours of Saturday morning.

Saturday sees the start of the football tournament - the Rentoy competition starts (card game) and the migas concorso starts lunchtime. I will explain. Migas is a breadcrumb dish similar to couscous, and is traditionally made with stale bread. In the old day's food was precious, and nothing was wasted. So, the idea of the competition is to cook the best migas on an open fire in the park. Well this leads to maybe sixty teams of cooks having a great party. Just like the Twickenham car parks before the rugby internationals. One-upmanship is the name of the game. Each team has a number which is attached to the pan for judging purposes. These days the migas is made from a semolina (semola) powder.

A couple of years ago we attended the fiesta and not being attached to a cooking team we were approached by one of the organisers (local policeman) who asked us to be judges. *What an honour*, we thought. We were led away to a massive pine tree where the pans of migas would be brought to be tasted and marked. Ample liquid refreshment was provided as you might expect. Well to be honest we can't stand the stuff. It's bland, has no particular taste, but to select the winner, each pan of nothingness had to sampled and awarded points on crumble, smoothness and presentation. One of the more street wise local hounds had noticed free food was available and he was visibly growing larger with every mouthful of red sausage (longaniza) used to adorn the pan. As the liquid refreshments took hold the judging became easier and with the assistance of the dog, we selected the winner.

After the fires were extinguished, the tables packed away and the last morsels of migas devoured, it is time for coffee and bingo. We all enjoy a game of bingo, so all the well fed and watered gathered in the marquee, paying two euros for a bingo card as Carmona's (local copper) helpers scurried around the tent selling the promise for great wealth ahead. The half-cut Carmona announces from the stage the amount to be won for a line and how much for a full house (casa) with great cheers from the awaiting audience. The bingo machine looks like it was bought in Toys R Us, but it does the business. Playing bingo in Spanish is a challenge, an even greater challenge when the caller is high on alcohol. Making a mistake is not an option, calling line or house and finding out you mistook sixty-six for seventy-six is slightly embarrassing. But tolerance is an enduring quality of the folk around here. As the game progresses the cost of the bingo card increases as well as the winnings. One old lady won four hundred and twenty euros, two tins of paint, a leg of jamon (preserved pork), a sack of dog food, a birdcage, ten litres of wine and a wheelbarrow. Lucky girl.

Sunday is the day of the parade. After mass rockets are fired off, not just a few but thousands, bursting into life with puffs of white smoke in the bright blue sky, the jettisoned sticks litter the pavements and are gathered up by gardeners for their tomatoes and the kids pick them up for the bike race later. Once the church bit is done it's back to the drinking, and lunch, with giant paella and beer for everyone. Nearly all of Órgiva decamp to Tablones for the Sunday. A local motorbike club turns up with huge bikes roaring like caged animals, and they set up their leg of jamon, pull out a huge knife and start slicing with such expertise the jamon is nearly transparent. It is quite amusing to see these leather-clad lads doing the paso-doble with their partners or any spare widow dressed in black. At the fiesta many years ago, a bunch of travelling musicians arrived and played stringed instruments all around the village. They turned out to be Dutch and were hired for the weekend.

After more bingo, it's time to bring San Marcos out of the church. With the Órgiva town band in attendance and the pealing of bells he appears at the church door carried by eight costaleros. Another crescendo of rockets and they make their way down the steps to the street all carefully choreographed and in step. The procession makes its way around the village boundary (similar to the beating of the bounds in England) with rockets flying in all directions. It's a lovely walk and can take an hour chatting away with our many Spanish friends on the route. As soon as San Marcos is safely back in the church the bike race for kids starts. They have a circuit of the village to take and a wire is strung across the street with ribbons (cintas) wound on. The idea is to hook a ribbon with your rocket stick as you ride your bike. If successful you earn the value of euros written on the ribbon, also you qualify for the piñata competition. They keep going around until all the ribbons have been claimed. A pinata is a clay pot full of sweets. The contestant is blindfolded and has to smash the pot with a hefty stick. Once broken, all the waiting kids dive in to grab as many sweets as possible. After all this excitement it must be time for another beer.

Carataunas is one of the smallest autonomous villages in Spain and the last census recorded 168 residents, yet it has its own town hall and mayor. San Marcos is celebrated here as well but not to such an extent as Tablones. A large paella, known in the area simply as Arroz, is cooked but no plates or cutlery are provided. The locals soon spy a stranger and furnish them with the correct implements. The famous cartoonist Martin Morales lives on the outskirts of the village, but sadly after an accident no longer takes part. They have a San Marcos day at the beginning of August, when a lot of sons and daughters return from exile for their holidays. In 2006 they had an evening of Flamenco, of course not starting until very late into the evening but perched on the Mirador overlooking Órgiva, it made a wonderful spectacle.

Self-Employed and Autonomous

THE FIRST TWELVE MONTHS INTO THE gamble went well with lots of paying guests (even Sarah's mother paid). It's great to see old friends who seem to come out of the woodwork when they learn you have a place in the sunshine in southern Spain, but why do they expect a free holiday? Not only are they taking up the space of a possible paying client but also, they expect to be wined, dined and entertained.

The medium we advertised the casitas in was traditional, a magazine called Community Care, the in-house rag for the Social Services. The previous owner used this method and it worked for her, so, if it's not broke don't fix it. We also went modern and used the web, when I was back in England packing up the house. I was on the phone to our friends in Devon who had farm letting cottages, and I asked them how they promoted their properties. They told me there is a web page called Devon Farmhouse holidays, and it gets them loads of enquiries. So, spanishfarmhouseholidays.co.uk was born. I checked the availability of the domain name and it was not registered. This gave us many bookings and also a great web page (although the name was a bit long) for potential clients to view and see what they were in for. The cost of renting the cottages was not high and this lured lots of lovely clients who respected the properties even though they all read the Guardian!

The extension was finished, and a wood-burning stove installed. We bought an expensive Norwegian model with a large door, so sensible sized logs would fit in. Most of the Spanish made wood burners were made of plate steel and would not be efficient, eating logs like sweets and not giving much heat back. Log burners with back boilers to heat water for domestic use or run radiators are not common here but some houses have them. The trouble with this form of heating is that it is not on demand and similar to looking after a baby, it constantly needs feeding and having its bottom cleaned!

So, we moved into the Casita Hoopoe, now two bedrooms, kitchen diner and a lounge. It was time to start renovating the other two. The letting season ran from Easter to the end of September and at Christmas, which meant we had time in the winter to get to work on improving the interiors of the casitas. Enquiries came in for long winter lets but people wanted to pay low rates, but it would cost us more in fuel and wear and tear on the houses as people spent more time indoors. Also, we had the work to do.

We renewed the kitchen in the Bee-eater and moved the kitchen in the Kingfisher, creating an extra bedroom. All the plumbing was renewed, and water heaters replaced.

It's most young families' dream to bring up their children in a rural environment. We sort of made a statement to ourselves when Alex was born, that we wanted our daughter to learn life skills like swimming, horse riding, holding a conversation with someone by listening and asking questions, being able to play a musical instrument, learning a foreign language, even ski. I think we have achieved most of this list. Having had a rural up bringing myself in a small farming town in Cornwall the chance to do the same for our daughter seemed like the right thing to do. What I didn't envisage was it was going to be in a foreign country. But in hindsight if I had to be a foreigner in another country then I would rather be a foreigner in Spain.

Child benefit is paid by the State when you have a child in the UK, this applies if you live in the UK. We called it our baby-sitting money to pay for baby-sitters when we went out. As we had left the UK, we stopped claiming it. This also means the mother of the child stops getting her national insurance paid which affects her pension when she gets to retirement age. In Spain you don't need baby-sitters as the child or children go out with you. In a very late bar in Órgiva which has a garden it is quite normal during the summer to see a pram or two at three o'clock in the morning! If you do have someone look after your children they are called Canguro´s (kangaroo).

Alex was settling in well at school and at play time, her group of friends consisted of locals as well as other foreign kids. We always said if she didn't settle then we would return to England. Alex didn't ask to join in the gamble, she didn't ask to join in the world she was being thrown into, but she accepted it and thrived.

The long summer school holidays need careful planning to keep your little ones occupied. Official swimming lessons take place at the municipal pool and summer camps are organised. Alex went on several of these camps and always came home with a bunch of new friends and stories to tell.

Having so much dry sunny weather, play time was always outside, not stuck in front of a play station or her parents being afraid to let her out on to the streets. We decided that a normal family life and routine should be stuck to. She saw us going to work every day, she knew weekdays were from Monday to Friday, weekends were for enjoyment and relaxation and going on holiday was part of the annual routine. Yes, just because you live in a sunny climate you still need a change of environment and something to look forward to.

Our first real holiday during our time in Spain was a cruise but having never been on one before we did not know what to expect. The ship was sailing from Malaga to Gibraltar, Tangier, Lanzarote, Tenerife, Madeira and then back to Malaga. I drove to the port in Malaga, there was no security so we just drove through the port gates and headed for the ship. Pulling up beside the embarkation steps a steward opened up the boot of the car and took our cases.

I asked, "Where should I park?"

He said, "Just over there will be fine."

"I hope we come back to the same dock."

The next morning, we arrived at Gibraltar and it was Alex's birthday. November the fourth. A trip around the rock and all its incredible history absorbed, visiting the apes and having your chocolate stolen by one of the little devils, then back on the ship and it was off to Africa. Two continents in one day and on your birthday, not bad. Tangier is not the best place to get introduced to Morocco. A guided tour of the souk and various unwanted purchases, like an authentic Jallabiya for Alex. Later I found myself face to face with the Moroccan guide and his mates demanding a very substantial tip. They realised quite rapidly they were going to be out of luck this time. Different continent or not, no bunch of punks were going to intimidate me.

Going on a cruise is like have a tasting menu, each of the destinations could be sampled and assessed for maybe a future holiday. Tenerife did it for us and we have returned several times since. The cruise was only seven days but enough time to put on a couple of kilos. Sure, enough on our return to Malaga the ship pulled up to the dock where the car was. Most of our fellow passengers had to catch a flight back to the UK, we just got in our car and drove home.

On another such trip I was going back to the UK to take my motorbike licence, a ten-day intensive course. Alex and I went and left Sarah in charge. Staying with some friends, we went to play some squash. Alex was happy playing on the kids' soft toy stuff, but afterwards in the bar she needed some fuel. Pistachios? Drinking my beer, I suddenly noticed people staring. Alex was tucking into her snack and dropping the shells onto the floor.

"No, you can't do that here."

"Why not, that's what we do in Spain?"

Driving test passed and we headed down to Devon to visit Alex's godmother on the farm. This was great as Aunty Jo had horses and Alex could show off her riding skills that she had learnt at the riding school, Caballo Blanco (white horse) high above Lanjaron. Confusion then reigned as we went off to watch Uncle Phil play cricket. You try describing the game of cricket to an eight-year-old. In the pub afterwards, we were sat down discussing googlies and off breaks.

"Could I have a drink please, Daddy?"

"Of course, go and ask the barman."

She came back in tears. "He won't even acknowledge me."

So, I went and had a little chat with the barman.

"Sorry, mate, can't serve children."

My reply was, "Well at least you can acknowledge they exist."

That highlights a big difference between the Spanish and the English. On a further visit to England with some Spanish friends we met up with a family in a pub on the Mendips, and we had to drink and eat in the children's room at the back of the pub. I showed Miguel around the ancient pub and he noticed a couple of old timers sat near the roaring fire with their collie dogs at their feet.

"You let dogs into pubs but not children! Strange lot you Brits!"

Here in Spain, in bars and restaurants you generally pay for what you have had at the end of your session. It's quite amusing picking up your drinks in England and walking away to your table with the bar person fussing because you didn't pay on the spot.

It is worth mentioning at this point that moving to a foreign country does not mean any marital problems you had when living in England disappear, you do not leave your shit behind you, it comes with you as well. Also, you will spend a lot more time in each other's company as you could and will be working together.

It was time for an adventure up the mountain. Alex had long school days on Monday and Tuesdays, so it gave us a window to have a look around. Some friends had suggested a track above Cana that led to a recreation area called Puente Palo, so with the trailer on and a full tank of diesel, a picnic and plenty of water, we set off. It was late November and we thought we could gather some fallen firewood and some pine cones, which make excellent firelighters. The road to Cana was very twisty but tarmac, but once through the village the track became rough and bumpy with numerous hairpin bends. There had been a snow fall during the night and the mountain above, Pico Rotundo, resembled a freshly iced cup cake.

Stopping frequently to fill the trailer with fallen chestnut boughs and anything else that looked compostable, we had to stop and take in the view. We pinched ourselves, wondering what the hell we were doing on a working Tuesday taking in panoramas of such stunning proportions which you could only imagine seeing in magazines advertising trekking holidays in the Austrian Tirol. The mountains in front of us looked like they were created by contortion and twisted, not born with grace but extruded by force. When we reached the track to turn right to Puente Palo, there was no track to be seen, it was covered in a blanket of fresh snow and we were the first vehicle to break its crust.

"Do you know where we are going?" Sarah asked.

"No, but I think it will be OK."

At 1,795 metres above sea level (Snowdonia is 1,085) exploring virgin territory is quite exciting, much better than talking to depressed farmers back in Somerset. We made it through the forest of pine trees following the gurgling acequia and as water flows downhill, I was confident we were heading in the right direction. Stopping for lunch, gazing at the sparkling Mediterranean way below us and again thinking, this isn't half bad for a Tuesday. Every thirty metres or so the views change and as the sun sinks for the day the shade on the mountain gullies make the hill sides move with different colours. An artist's paradise.

On the way down the mountain towards Soportujar we passed a track with a sign informing us of the whereabouts of the Buddhist retreat of O Sei Ling. I had heard there was such a place in the locality, so we made a mental note to explore this strange location for Buddhism another day.

At one thousand six hundred metres above sea level and perched on a remote mountain side this Buddhist retreat began life in 1982, but you have to ask yourself, why? The connection between this Buddhist site and Tibet started in the eighties when a two-year-old boy from Granada was confirmed by the Dalai Lama to be a reincarnation in Tibetan Buddhism. They believed he was the reincarnation of the extrovert Tibetan Lama Yeshe. They called the boy Tenzin Osel Rinpoche. The first Spanish child to be recognised as a Lama. There are over twenty Buddhist sites throughout Spain.

When Osel was a small boy he was taken to southern India for evaluation by Buddhist monks. Part of this evaluation was to select some of Lama Yeshe's possessions, and this he did despite having never met the man. After this he lived in a southern Indian Buddhist monastery. When he was nine his father and brother joined him and they returned to Spain when he was eighteen. The retreat O Sei Ling means a place of clear light. The first year we were here I was invited to join in a sponsored walk raising money to help Tibetan orphans. The final destination was to be the meditation hall in O Sei Ling.

This sounds interesting, I thought.

The distance of the hike was only ten kilometres over gentle countryside. With a packed lunch and a few beers in my rucksack, we all set off. Sarah declined the walk. My fellow hikers were very much from the alternative brigade; but it was good to get to know a few of them. Arriving at the sacred site we all gathered in the hall, sitting on the floor to share our offerings. The guy to my right was horrified when I offered him one of my ham and pickle sandwiches and a tin of beer. I had to eat my lunch on my own outside. I didn't know, did I? The retreat offers a time for spiritual solitude, a time for reflection, prayer and meditation. It will shut out the noise in your life and other distractions, and you will come face to face with yourself and cost you six hundred euros for a week. The centre is now mainly run by women and a huge hostel is now being built in the middle of Órgiva to accommodate the families of the monks.

Life progressed at a whirlwind pace, one minute it is Monday the next Friday. New skills were being learnt every day: plumbing, electrical installations, tiling and even my pet hate, car mechanics. Our Spanish vocabulary was expanding but mainly in the context of the work we were undertaking and what we were eating and drinking. On some occasions getting the two mixed up. The block and beam roofing system consist of a beam (viga) and the block (bovedilla). The word for meatball is Albondiga. I got the two mixed up. Asking a waiter for a ration of bovedillas got a very strange reply and a good laugh as well. Also discussing the virtues of the Landrover against the Japanese four by fours, I said Landrovers don't like pavo (turkey) in their radiators. I should have said polvo (dust). Polvo is also Spanish slang for having sex!

Having decided that we were staying and putting down roots in this wonderful part of Andalucía it was time to sell the house in England and get the mortgage paid off again! The gamble just got serious. This did not take long as Evercreech is a very nice village and our type of property was in demand. Our fantastic solicitor, Robin sorted out all the paperwork and deposited a healthy-looking cheque into our English bank account after the mortgage and his fees were paid. Okay, the pressure was off now and life should be a little more relaxed. Wrong. Sarah had spied an attractive piece of land close to our casitas with a ruin on it.

"I wonder what sort of money that would sell for, if it came on the market? It's so close to us we could move up there during the busy season, live in the caravan and rent all three cottages out."

I agreed it was a fine parcel of land, not too big and the ruin should make it easier to get permission to repair it. But it's not for sale. Wrong again. Our neighbour, Eric, who could speak Spanish, popped up as he did normally when he wanted something.

"I hear that piece of land is for sale opposite us." It is normal in Spain that if you are selling a property or land you inform your neighbours first.

That's a coincidence, I thought.

So, a meeting was arranged with Manolo, the property owner's son.

On inspection, it was flat, had good access, lots of acequia rights, no electric or town water, but it was all very close to be connected!

The price of the land was five million pesetas, twenty thousand pounds. We shook hands and we were off to the notaria again. A deposit is normally paid, ten per cent.

Manolo took his wallet out and said, "This is my bank," meaning he wanted cash.

Off to the bank to collect five hundred thousand pesetas.

"No hay," (I don't have it) the bank teller said. "One moment please," she said. She picked up a receipt book and a carrier bag and off she went to the other banks in town and within ten minutes she returned with a bag full of notes.

The deposit was paid and a date set for the completion, and the balance of the cash pre-ordered in the bank, so there would be no more running around collecting four and a half million pesetas and within three weeks we owned our second property in Spain. Having paid Manolo his money he took us to another bank and paid the money (cash) into his mother's account. This was a head scratcher, had he never heard of a bank transfer? We had a celebratory drink with him and his mother and the normal saying, 'I have given you a gift'. And do you know what? He had!

Our daughter, Alex was enjoying school. The educational system in Spain is different than in England. At the beginning of the new school year you are given a list of the work books your child will need, and a list of the consumables needed: paper, pens, pencils, folders. There is no black hole in Spanish schools for materials to disappear. This list could mount up to a couple of hundred euros worth. It was a bit of a shock the first year. Often, she would return from school with bright orange knees, Betadine was the answer to any scrape or graze from the gravel covered play area.

Mondays and Tuesdays were long days and lunch was provided by the school for those who lived out of town. It was nearly two years before we found out that Alex did not like the school food and that she had been going to a Spanish friend's place for lunch. Embarrassed, we apologised to the mother who just shrugged and said, "What's one more mouth to feed." The school bus did not come down our road and so we took her to school every day, and with no school uniform to wear it was always a difficult fashion choice in the mornings. We received a cheque in the post from the school authority paying us, as no school transport was available for our part of the campo.

The schooling was old fashioned, sit at the desk and look at the blackboard. Often kids would get a clip across the ear for misbehaving. On one such incident Alex's zip had got stuck on her jumper so she was taking it off over her head. She received a hard belt over her head and assumed it was the teacher. A complaint from me went to the headmaster. Sarah was in England attending a funeral. We were summoned to a meeting with the headmaster and asked what proof did she have it was the teacher. None. He said teachers have rights too and suspended Alex for three days. Collecting Sarah from the airport, Alex came with me as she could not go to school. We were ten kilometres up the road before Sarah said, "Why are you not at school?"

Back down the road to Las Golondrinas the garden was in its prime with flowers popping up all over the place and a rich variety of herbs that I only thought came in little expensive bottles in the supermarket. Plumes of rosemary, sage, prostrate to the ground, marjoram fragrant to touch and an ever-growing supply of coriander for cooking with. Thyme, basil, bay, and kafia lime shrubs producing leaves for infusing Thai curries. All of this needed constant watering and the acequia of the Camino la Estrella did not let us down.

Thursday was our watering day and due to the engineering of the Moors, way back in the 12th century, it became an easy and satisfying thing to do. Everything was growing so fast that the garden was in need of a serious prune, it was more like entering a green cave. Then along came Baz, a Cornishman who knew a thing or two about pruning. We went away for the day leaving Baz to his own devices. On our return it looked like a tornado had ripped through the place. Sarah had tears in her eyes.

"Don't worry, my lover, it will grow back stronger and at least now you can see the mountains," Baz assured her.

I said, "Where are we going to burn all that lot?" You need permission to burn and it normally runs from November to April depending on the weather. I had a sound business idea and that would be to purchase a tree surgeon grade chipper and tractor and mash up garden waste into mulch. This was vetoed by Sarah, so I still didn't have my tractor.

The land and ruin we had bought was called Cortijo La Era, named after a crop drying circle by the house. These drying platforms are always built where a good breeze occurs and can be found all over the Alpujarras. They are normally placed much higher in the mountains where the barley, wheat and oats are grown.

Once the crop is placed on the stone slabs a donkey pulls a man riding on a sleigh around the circle separating the wheat from the chaff so to speak. Then the farmers would toss the harvested straw in the air and the wind blows away all the rubbish leaving the precious grain behind. Similar to a winnowing machine but not on wheels. Our stone circle was for broad beans, a good source of protein as animal feed and the plant fixes nitrogen into the soil as it grows as an added bonus.

The land we had bought had some English neighbours to our left and Spanish to our right. The English neighbours were great people, very helpful. Andrew approached me one day asking if they could use our land to access the back of his garden as they wanted to build a one-bedroomed casita there.

"No problem, I could assist with supplying the material."

Access was a bit tight for a lorry to deliver. His builder, Juan, was a great bloke. He pulled me to one side and suggested that with a digger for an hour the access could be improved and if we uprooted a couple of almond trees, we could have all the materials at hand. I pointed out that I would be putting myself out of a job.

"No, you won't," he said. "You can work with us, looks like you can handle a shovel."

Like a dog with two tails I told Sarah I had a paid job working for Juan. The first guiri (what the locals call us northern Europeans) in the area to get a job working for a Spanish builder. As I laboured, I watched and learnt. My fellow labourer was a young Spanish lad called Miguel, who was very wiry and had the piss taken out of him on a constant basis by his elder Spanish builder mates. Some years later I met him at a fiesta, now filled out with a muscular physique on a broad pair of shoulders. He was proud to show me a photo of himself in a smart Guardia Civil uniform. I was very glad my Spanish was not good enough when working with him to have joined in with the mickey taking.

We decided to apply for permission to reform the ruin, build an alberca (swimming pool), a garden wall and repair the Era (an item of historical importance). Having a chat with my Spanish builder friend he suggested we start as the permission could take a while and it would be better to start work before the heat of the summer arrived. The first job was to take the roof off. This consisted of a grey clay called launa, a natural waterproofing substance dug from the mountain side. Next was cardboard covered in dry herbs (to keep the wood eating insects at bay) and then the eucalyptus beams harvested from the nearby woods. I don't know how long they had been in place, but they were still sound and strong. As long as they are kept dry the beams will last forever. The width of most local farmhouse rooms and town houses is determined by the beams that are available. A four-metre beam is about the norm. So, the rooms are three metres wide. Once the roof was off the walls became very unstable and collapsed (that's my story and I'm sticking to it). So, now we had a pile of river stones instead of a ruin.

Living and working in Spain gives you great pleasures, one of them that is not a pleasure is paying the national insurance contributions. Autonomo. Whatever work you choose to do means being self-employed. Very few Spanish companies will employ foreign workers. So, self-employment is the only way if you want to be legal.

Each type of work has a different risk level, this is reflected in how much you pay. They are known as modelos. Being a builder means paying in excess of three-hundred euros a month. This gives your health cover (for the whole family) and a pension (third worst in EEC, Romania is the worst). What I did not realise was that when my accountant signed me on to be autonomo she tagged on a separate health insurance which was to prove very beneficial when my hip needed replacing, but that's another story.

The year is split into four, three-month periods called, trimesters. They start from January. At the end of each trimester you have to supply information to your accountant, with receipts from items purchased. They must be personal to you, your Numero de Identidad de Extranjero (N.I.E.) on the receipt. This can prove to be a difficult request to satisfy.

Petrol, cash till receipts, no good. Mobile phone pays as you go, no chance. Internet costs, possible. Tools etc, a much better price if you pay in cash.

Any income from work must have IVA added onto your labour charge. Also, make sure your labour charge is sufficient to cover your national insurance cost.

So how much do you charge an hour? Let's say, basic cost per hour, ten euros, add on your NI. One point seven euros per hour. Plus, IVA, at twenty-one percent, two euros forty-six cent, so now your ten euros is now fourteen euros forty-six cents.

If you added on your administration costs, accountant's fees (don't ask for an official receipt, cash is better) although I was told to collect as many official receipts as possible, your hourly rate should be sixteen euros.

You try getting work at that rate and pro rata. Hence the labour vacuum with Romanian workers filling the void helped by the fact that the Romanian language is very similar to Spanish. But it was time to start paying my contributions as we were staying and in hindsight it was one of the best decisions we made. Living and working in a European country does not mean you can dodge paying into the local or national system. Spain was educating our daughter and we had the health service at our disposal.

Everything was going fine until my hip replacement started to become very painful. I had my right hip replaced in 1989 in Yeovil, Somerset. I was at the tender age of thirty, very early in life for such an operation but the pain it was putting me through then left me with no option. I suppose moving to Spain was part of the recovery therapy, a warmer less damp climate, away from temptation to put on the rugby boots. But life in Spain was far more physical than I envisaged. I did not expect to build our own house or get involved in many other building projects. But in 2012 after twenty-four years my prothesis was beginning to come loose so another hip replacement to replace the replacement was on the cards, Spanish style.

After several x-rays and scans I was booked in for the operation after only four months from the initial problem beginning. April 2013 in Motril. New Spanish words were being added to my vocabulary, medical ones.

Quirofano sticks in the mind as I passed out from the anaesthetic, it means operating theatre. The operation went well and after five days I was back home on my muletas (crutches). I found the whole procedure very efficient, it's a modern health service with plenty of well-trained staff, very clean, and the food was excellent. The Spanish say in Motril hospital you get excellent fish (as it's a fishing port) and Granada you get good beef as the hospital is close to the bull ring! But some things are slightly different to the UK. There were two beds in my ward. An older guy was in for a new knee, he had his son stay with him every night, snoring louder than his dad, as the family do a lot of the nursing. On the Sunday it was more like a party in my room, he must have had twenty visitors. They sat on my bed, had a good chat with me and shared their wine. Don't tell matron! Walking aids such as crutches and any other mobility machines have to be supplied by the patient. On a more serious note the aftercare was not good, you need to organise your own physiotherapy and rehabilitation.

The education system is efficient and compulsory for all children resident in Spain. Home education is not illegal in Spain but not many parents take this option. There are plenty of pre-school kindergarten nurseries. Primary school runs from the age of six to twelve years of age, and is run on three two-year cycles, and repeating a year is necessary if the student does not reach the approved standard. Secondary school is up to the age of sixteen and now runs on a more relaxed system akin to the British comprehensive system. Continuous assessment and project work. Religious education is optional. You then can leave or go on to take the Bachillerato (A levels). Lots of homework is handed out at all ages.

The Bachillerato is based on nine subjects and when the certificate is achieved university entrance is possible, although an entrance exam will need to be passed as well.

Alex's choice for her two-year Bachillerato course was art based, this was not available in Orgiva, but she could study this option in Granada. A grant was available to cover her accommodation and travel costs. After the two years she passed her exams and decided to study interior design, another two-year course and again grant aided. When she graduated, she was qualified with no debt or overdraft. Another year studying the CAD computer system allowed her to be able to draft and draw plans for building projects, very useful. On reflection, paying autonomo is well worth it. A successful gamble for once.

Easter. Semana Santa
La Pascua

THE MOST IMPORTANT RELIGIOUS OCCASION THROUGHOUT all of Spain. Easter week starts on the Sunday before Easter. Palm Sunday, Passion Sunday or Ramos Sunday, the day Jesus entered Jerusalem riding a donkey, with the crowds waving palm leaves and olive branches in the air at him. In Órgiva the congregation from the church walk up to the cross in front of the Guardia Civil barracks carrying their palm fronds and olive twigs and the priest performs a service, a hymn is then sung while returning to the church. This happens during the last week of Lent.

Lent starts on Ash Wednesday and continues for forty days until Easter Saturday. Holy Wednesday (spy Wednesday) when Judas was arranging his betrayal of Jesus for the thirty pieces of silver. He tried to hand the silver back after the betrayal, but it was not accepted so he hung himself of a tree now called the Judas tree. Maundy Thursday the day of the last supper. Good Friday commemorates the day of the crucifixion of Jesus and his subsequent death.

In the large cities of Andalucía processions take place every day during this week. Thousands of people flock to watch these massive catafalques adorned with huge idols and carried by sometimes more than a hundred costaleros. Remember the bit about the size of the church doors!

In Órgiva the church doors are quite small so the size of the catafalque for the Thursday parade, Jesus carrying his cross, is impressive but somewhat smaller than that of Granada. A much more solemn occasion than El Cristo. Theatre being the theme. All the members of the Brotherhood of Nazareno are attired in the purple associated with the impending crucifixion. The capirotes (pointed conical hats) reach into the sky towards heaven like the cypress trees you see around graveyards. The carefully choreographed movement of the platform with the condemned figure aboard makes its way slowly towards that hill. A visiting band from Alcala Real follow the platform along with the hundred or so penitents ranging in age from three-year-olds to veterans. The capirotes they wear cover their identity so as they are serving their penitence immunity remains.

The Friday procession, our Brotherhood, Dolores and the Sepulchre, have white robes and white pointed hats and black velvet cloaks that do resemble the Ku Klux Klan but that's as far as it goes (it's more like something out of Harry Potter). At 10pm we carry out of the church, Jesus in his glass coffin and the Virgin Dolores. The town band is behind us playing solemn music and on our route a lady will suddenly appear from nowhere and sing the lament of Saeta. It's quite a scary song when you are not expecting it. The costaleros do not have the pointed hats on as trying to pick up and manoeuvre the platform would be even more difficult than it already is. As the temperature increases the white silk sticks to your face and with two small eye holes to see through this makes navigation difficult. The answer is a small pair of ski googles with the glass taken out, this keeps the silk away from your face. One year I did not carry so I volunteered to take some photos, it was quite amusing when they wanted their pictures taken, as they were all wearing hoods, who was who?

During the four days of Easter, Thursday through to Sunday an Artisan fair is held in the big green hall next to the sports complex. Hecho en La Alpujarras (made in the Alpujarras). Local products to sample and buy such as wonderful wine from the Four Winds bodega, Murtas situated high on the Contrevisa Mountain range overlooking the Mediterranean sea, cheese produced from the local sheep and goats' milk, bread baked in wood ovens, beer from the micro-brewery in Lanjaron, jamon (air dried ham) from the drying houses high up in the clean air of the Sierra Nevada, dried and cured sausages (embutidos) of all types made locally, olive oil from the ancient olive trees of Órgiva, chocolate made in Pampaneira with flavours to tickle your fancy, chocolate with cracked black pepper, chocolate with mango, chocolate with mandarin and even chocolate that tastes like chocolate. Honey produced from the year-round blossom we are so lucky to witness. Turron (nougat) made from the almonds of the Alpujarras and the honey from the hives of the area. You can hear the hammer and chisel breaking up the mass of nougat from a distance, so imagine what it does to your teeth. A dentist's dream, so if you have fragile teeth beware! At lunch time (2pm) bread is purchased and plates of jamon, salami, morcilla (blood sausage) and dried pork loin are devoured with a few beers, finished off with some sweet treats from the various stalls selling their own creations. The word for home-made in Spanish is casera.

There are hand crafted items made from leather, pottery from Las Barreras, wood turned from olive, mulberry and other exotic species into beautiful bowls, lamps, pens and even beer bottles! Art from the many local artists, brilliantly coloured rugs made in the famous white villages of the Alpujarras. Herbalists selling the magic potions that promise a cure even Peter Pan would be interested in. Soaps and creams with olive oil in the list of ingredients. Woven baskets made out of Esparto grass. It is an exhibition well worth a visit. Easter is a silent celebration until Easter Sunday. Then mass rockets pepper the sky celebrating the resurrection and the start of the new Christian year.

On Easter Sunday the resurrection is celebrated. After mass at midday, a procession comprising of the three Brotherhoods make their way out of the church. The children carry a small platform with the virgin in prayer (start them young), and another platform with the resurrected Christ on board is carried by a selection of costaleros of the three Brotherhoods, white shirts being the order of the day. Prominent church leaders walk with their pastoral staffs, sometimes known as a crozier and the banners of the Brotherhoods. The madrinas have now changed their black mantillas and black gloves for white ones. As the two platforms emerge from the church rose petals float down from the church balcony. The congregation follows ringing small bells, but of course the odd joker follows with a cow bell!

Easter eggs are not common in this part of Spain, which is strange as local people from Órgiva are known as the egg people (hueveros). The history of giving eggs on Easter Sunday is a bit sketchy but it is meant to symbolize new life. Shrove Tuesday (pancake day), the day before the start of Lent is a day invented to use up all your eggs before the fast starts. In many parts of Europe eggs are dyed red to represent the blood of Christ. In Romania the red eggs are baked in a type of bread. Hot cross buns (panecello con cruz) are eaten on Good Friday. These comprise a spiced dough with raisins and a cross on the top, and their origins date back to pagan times, the cross representing the four phases of the moon and dedicated to the goddess Eostre (this is believed to be where the word Easter originates from).

Stmo. Cristo de la Expiracion
The Big Bang

TWO WEEKS BEFORE EASTER A CELEBRATION takes place in Órgiva that is unique in Spain. In 1599 a carved effigy of Christ on the cross was presented to the church of La Inglesia de Nuestra Senora de la Expectacion. The church of our Lady of the Expectation, Órgiva, and is now worshiped by the parishioners. In the town where I was born, Launceston, about the same size as Órgiva, there are eight places of worship. In Órgiva there is one. The Ermita of San Sebastian is not a regular place of worship. The cross and the figure of Christ is carved from cedar wood and is from the school of Juan Martinez Montanez, Granada. The cross is three metres high and nearly two metres wide. At the beginning of the week you are aware that something is about to take place as periodic bursts of rocket fire start to disrupt the peace, which even the noisy barking dogs can't compete with. The Thursday, two weeks before Easter Thursday, every year at midday, the effigy is carefully lifted off the high altar amid scenes of hysterical chanting and hand waving that makes the hairs on the back of your neck stand on end. This is called the la Bajada del Senor.

With the wonderful town band (known as Exoche, an old Greek name for Órgiva), playing melancholy tunes up in the gallery and all the pews cleared to the sides of the church, a throng of a couple of thousand souls congregate to watch the event. They gather at the church from all over the Alpujarras, with people returning from self-imposed exile to join in the celebrations and reunite with family and friends. A chain is attached to the top of the cross that helps lift and awaken the idol. From eleven-thirty in the morning mostly men from the Brotherhood of Cristo de la Expiracion (hermandades), enter the high altar through a secret door and wave and shout 'viva Cristo Expiracion' hands held in the air like a preacher from the deep south. The crowd respond with 'viva'. It feels like the people are taking back the church for the weekend.

The various Brotherhoods date back to the thirteenth century when men of the same trade formed unions to help keep the peace, vigilantes for the nobility. As they lost this role to proper law enforcers, they then became community leaders akin to Freemasons. These days for example in Seville you can find over 60 Brotherhoods scattered over the various parishes.

As midday approaches the crowd push to get as close to the front of the church as possible, with their phones held aloft recording as much detail as possible. It was streamed live on Facebook last year. The effigy is released from the altar and shaken from side to side and exactly at midday the 8,000 bangers (tracas) out on the street strung up like long lines of sausages, detonate a salvo that scares the birds from the trees. Meanwhile, the town band play La Marcha Real, the national anthem of Spain, and the church bells ring out for all they are worth.

The national anthem of Spain is thought to be one of the oldest in the world. It is one of only four national anthems worldwide not to have any words. The other three are Bosnia and Herzegovina, Kosovo and San Marino. Since 1978 the words were banned as the words paid homage to Franco's ideology.

The effigy on the cross now sort of crowd surfs over people's heads until it comes to the base of the catafalque to which it will be attached upright for the forthcoming procession. The statue is cleaned by anybody that can reach, with white hankies bringing them good luck for the coming year. People are crying and shuddering with passion as they get reborn trying to leave the church through a very small door, until the police open up the large exit. All the bars in town do a roaring trade as taking part in the Bajada is thirsty work, and most locals take the rest of the day off. Tomorrow is a local holiday and will be bigger and better.

The statue of Christ is in the care of the Brotherhood of the Holy Christ of Expiration. It might preside in the church but the Brotherhood look after it. It has been restored many times as the polychrome paintwork gets worn by the constant rubbing and kissing by the devotees of the parish. The prestigious restorer of works of art, Dioniso Olgoso Moreno of Motril, last restored the valuable statue in 2017 coming to the church every day for a month to do his work. The biggest threat to any of these cherished effigies sculptured from wood is the Xylophagous beetle. The same real threat that you can hear munching away at your wooden roof beams. The silver crown that adorns the head of the statue after the Bajada was gifted in 1855 by the Areanas family, great devotees of the Holy Christ of Expiration, was restored in 1915 and it is the job of two brothers of the family to polish the crown so it sparkles for the following day.

During the Thursday evening the catafalques of Christ and that of the Virgin de los Dolores are prepared for the procession the following day. Two thousand red carnations (the flower of Spain) and a thousand white carnations are used to decorate both floats. Red for Cristo and white for the Virgin Dolores. The cost of the flowers alone to decorate her float comes to over 1,000 euros.

Ornate lamps with hidden battery packs, which will light up the statues for the long procession to come are put in place. Plastic see-through covers are secreted in the undercarriage in case of rain.

The Brotherhood of the Virgin de los Dolores and the Holy Sepulchre (also known as the Cofradia), are responsible for the decoration and upkeep of the Lady of Sorrows. Her wonderful cloak and jewels are a spectacle to behold. The Virgin Mary has many different titles, Dolores is one of them. The seven sorrows of Mary are as follows; The prophecy of Simeon; (Lola is a short name of Dolores). The escape and flight into Egypt; the loss of the Child Jesus in the temple of Jerusalem; The meeting of Mary and Jesus on the Via Dolorosa; The Crucifixion of Jesus on Mount Calvary and the piercing of the side of Jesus with a spear and his descent from the cross.

Her rosary, chaplet is of the seven sorrows, consisting of seven black wooden beads separated with a metal disc.

Friday is the most important religious day of the whole year in Órgiva. At dawn a salvo of rockets awakens the town like a twenty-one-gun salute. The first mass is at nine o'clock followed by the next at twelve and the eucharist is sung by the great choirs of Órgiva. Another 8,000 explosions hammer away in the high street after the service. The smartly dressed devoted parishioners retire for lunch and get prepared for the evening's processions. The church is again cleared of all the pews and becomes a great hall. Christ is positioned to the left facing the church doors and Dolores to his right both high on their podiums looking down at the gathering throng.

From five o'clock in the afternoon and all preparations complete, and with appetites and thirst quenched, the town fills up with thousands of people. Security is tight and the dress code is smart. The military band of the Spanish Foreign Legion are blowing their bugles and the drummers smashing out the beat. Choreographed soldiers march up and down the street with rifles twirling followed by the regimental mascot, a goat.

In the church the town band are behind the two statues and the costaleros gather for the impending ten-hour procession. The costaleros are the teams of people who have been trained to carry the effigies. The team who carry the statue of Christ are a scruffy bunch who jostle and shove each other to be in the best position for the exodus from the church. The team that carry the Virgin are all dressed in smart dark navy-blue suits, white shirts, black ties and black shoes. White gloves covering their hands and the medallion of the Virgin Dolores around their necks give themselves a look of respectability. Twelve costaleros carry the Virgin, and they are carefully selected for their height and given the position that suits their gait. Two teams are used for the long procession, swapping over at around ten o'clock. Training for the event can start ten weeks before and includes precision lifting and dance movements to a particular musical piece performed by the town band. The musical piece is called El Cristo de las Aguas.

The military band is now inside the church, along with the goat and many hundreds of onlookers (sorry, devotees), and the band is making one heck of a din with every conceivable type of brass instrument available. Christ goes first, with a slow march towards the doors with the foreman at the front of the catafalque controlling the pace. Aiming to get to the church doors spot on six, the military band provide a guard of honour. The Virgin Dolores is now following with the priest, his junior, the mayoress and captain of the Guardia Civil closely in attendance. The costaleros not carrying form their own guard of honour for the Lady of Sorrows. The madrinas (godmothers) form a line each carrying a bouquet of flowers and dressed in black with their mantillas high above their heads, and some actually weeping. These women also belong to the Cofradia of Dolores.

When Christ enters into the daylight at exactly six pm the whole town erupts into the loudest burst of explosions you will hear outside of a war zone. The street once again has over 10,000 tracas strung up and exploding like dancing marionettes, thousands of rockets (cohetes) fly into the sky leaving puffs of smoke before the sound reaches the speechless audience. This racket goes on for at least ten minutes covering the whole town in a blanket of smoke and the smell of cordite and saltpetre fills the air. With a blink of the eye the pyrotechnic teams have cleared the street of all the debris allowing the military band to parade and play while Cristo is brought with great care down the church steps onto the street to vigorous applause and more 'viva el senor' and 'viva'. The street becomes an improvised stage with sub-divisions unfolding before the audience's eyes. The Virgin now makes her way to the church doors after some kind soul has cleaned up the mess that the goat left behind. The town band are now in full flow playing El Cristo de las Aguas and the costaleros performing the practiced dance in time to the music while carrying nearly a tonne of carriage, flowers, batteries and her Lady. No easy task. She is now out into the sunlight and on her way down the steps to take her place alongside El Cristo both facing up the street. The madrinas now present the floral gifts before the procession sets off.

Mourners make a line on each side of the street holding candles for later on. Cristo goes first followed by the military band with more sporadic rockets being let off. Dolores follows again with the town band close behind. Progress is slow as at each important crossroads a cleansing has to take place with Catherine wheels set off and more explosions. Imitating the fourteen Stations of the Cross. This allows the costaleros to take a well-deserved rest, check their phones and light up.

Along the route houses are open for a quick comfort break and a sneaky coffee or something stronger. The narrow streets prove a tricky route and vigilance is needed in case a low cable has been strung across the street since last year. Garrotting the Virgin would not be popular. Postcards are handed out to the lucky few bearing the latest picture of the Virgin which they wipe on her velvet cloak for luck. To own a property on the route is important to the people in the know and their value reflects this. By ten o'clock they have reached the market square and a change of teams takes place and a very nice colourful firework display lasting twenty minutes illuminates the night's sky. Then it's off again to make the arduous climb to the sixteenth century Ermita of San Sebastian. It's just as arduous coming down the steep hill as it is going up. The procession is now on the home run back to the church. Calle Libertade - all Spanish towns and cities have a Calle Libertade, although they used to be called Calle Franco. The time for the return to the church varies depending on how many people follow Christ and how long the frequent explosions take. But normally two am is about right. Once back in front of the church steps the two statues line up together and another fantastic pyrotechnic display happens. First Christ is taken in up the steps and then the Virgin, both backwards, returning to the altar. A mad scramble then takes place to grab a carnation from each catafalque. Receiving red carnations means my heart aches for you and white carnations means luck. Legend has it that the first carnation appeared on earth as Mary wept for Jesus as he carried his cross on his way to Mount Calvary.

The following Saturday at noon the Subida del Stmo. Cristo de la Expiracion de Altar al Camarin takes place as he is lifted once again up into the altar to take his rightful place in time for Easter. Of course, another 8,000 tracas explode outside to mark the occasion.

During our first spring in Órgiva we were informed of this event and were keen to observe. We got into town early on the Friday afternoon, taking our place outside the Bar Paradise opposite the church, next to the chemists with the Durex vending machine on the wall and were dressed somewhat inappropriately in touristy looking clothes. The locals started arriving all dressed in their Sunday best with even the youngsters sporting the latest fashion. I nearly went home and changed. Instead I made a mental note that next year would be different. All the tracas (bangers) were in place and as six o'clock approached the barman dragged us inside and told us to open our mouths to equalise the pressure when they started exploding otherwise our eardrums would be damaged. One year the explosions were so fierce the window of the bank blew out and a man had to have his leg amputated due to his injuries. The procession that year returned to the church at two-thirty Saturday afternoon.

Órgiva has a large population of alternative living people of all types and ideas. A festival established itself to celebrate the spring equinox, the Dragon festival. This was based in the river bed near the hamlet of Cigarones. Unfortunately, this often clashed with the El Cristo celebrations. The tolerant folk of Órgiva put up with this invasion of thousands of festival goers at a time when many normal Christian devotees were visiting the town. Obviously, it had its financial benefits and the supermarkets did a roaring trade in festival refreshments. A few attempts were made to make the festival illegal and get it banned but, in the end, nature provided the solution. The town hall along with medioambiente (environmental agency) approved a tree planting scheme on the festival site. Diggers moved in to provide the holes for the saplings, and after the heavy torrential rains of the winter of two thousand and ten the river burst its banks and flooded the whole site sweeping away houses, vans, lorries, caravans and anything else that got in its way and filling up the intended holes for the trees with water making the area very dangerous. The Dragon festival was cancelled and the next year moved to a site near Granada to the relief of the town hall but not the supermarket owners.

The following year and being dressed more appropriately for the occasion and after we had witnessed the Virgin of Sorrows ascend the church steps, Juan, the president of the Cofradia, beckoned me to come over.

He said, "I think you have the right height and strength to help us next year, would you be interested in joining the Brotherhood?"

I replied, "It would be a great honour." So, the following year I entered the Cofradia of the Virgin de los Dolores and the Holy Sepulchre.

Training began on one Saturday evening in the middle of January. Eight weeks before the procession. We had been to a barbeque all afternoon and a few beers had been drunk to dull the pain of the forthcoming torture. Alex, my daughter, came with me to translate the instructions. On a deserted, well-lit street outside Juan's house we all gathered, eventually. Six taller guys on the front and six shorter ones on the back (that's where I came in). With no Virgin on her throne and no batteries the catafalque was not as heavy as I would have imagined.

Alex was now invited to sit on the platform so she could relay the instructions shouted out by the foreman to her slightly inebriated daddy. An elaborate brass door knocker on the front carrying pole also gave notice of an imminent manoeuvre. This is essential during the parade as the noise from the bands and the rockets can drown out the loudest of voices, so the knocker reverberates through the structure informing us all of upcoming activity. El Cristo uses a bell. Get ready, one knock, two knocks, down on one knee ready to lift, on the next knock, all lift together. Up went the platform like a wobbling jelly. Up and down the wooden platform went until like military precision we all worked together raising it as one. With a shout of 'vamos' we lurched forward walking down the street. 'Mass despacio' (slow down) came the call, slower, stop, put her down, pick her up and so on. Iparo, Iquado, el brazo, derecha, izquierda. All instructions that needed to be learnt.

Eventually the first practice was over, cigarettes were lit and cans of beer handed out and telephones checked; I think due to my military training (air cadets at school) I picked it up quite well. How much I would remember for the next practice we would have to wait and see. It was soon Wednesday and practice time again. Tonight, was not just up and down, walking, stopping, it had a dance movement introduced, the Sevianno. More and more costaleros appeared, some I knew and some total strangers, but all of them accepted me as a friend and a member of the team. The hierarchy of the Brotherhood soon became apparent; the president and two foremen were top dogs, below that was us lot. Cannon fodder. One evening Juan asked if I was enjoying myself and was I serious about joining. I thought here comes the initiation. What's it going to be? A bare left breast, drinking some horrible concoction, eating twenty morcilla (black pudding akin to a soggy dog turd), no he just wanted 50 euros for the annual subscription. I was told where to buy my navy-blue suit and where to go to get measured for my Semana Santa cloak and pointy-head gear called a capirote or a coroza. During the inquisition people were made to wear these pointed hats as a sign of public humiliation.

As the weeks went by practice became more enjoyable and more sociable, my Spanish improving by integration. Practice moved from the quite suburban road to the centre of the town, traffic was made to wait as we marched up and down the various streets. A couple of new arrivals to Órgiva who were renting a flat until their cortijo was available were on their balcony, "Kev, come look at this, there are twelve blokes stealing a table with a door knocker on it." Said Fe.

Some tapas started appearing as well to go with the beer and wine afterwards, and one-upmanship kicked in, but the snails in a lovely almond spicy sauce won, although it was a little too spicy for some. They don't like it hot.

The celebration of El Senor de la Expiracion came around much quicker than I expected, and a meeting was called in the church, deep in the bowels of the building. The priest gave us a lecture about the importance of the celebration and then followed the team selections for the procession. I had made it into the second shift at the back under the Virgin's cloak! What was an Englishman doing in this position?

We all had to meet at the church five o'clock sharp on the Friday and sober. The madrinas (godmothers) were asked to rehearse so the older ones could show the little ones what to do. More familiar faces started to appear, and I found out the membership exceeded four hundred. Different annual subscriptions for different roles. Money has to be raised as the Cofradia pays for the flowers, the hiring of the town band, the printing of the postcards with the latest photo of the Virgin, renting the garage where the paraphernalia is stored, the Harry Potter type cloaks for Easter and for the feast of Dolores on the Friday before Easter after the mass in honour of her name. Over 6,000 euros per year in total is needed.

Five o'clock on the Friday I met Juan in the bar as arranged, a very swift gin and tonic, no beer as pee stops are few and far between and it was off to the church in through a back door thus avoiding the crowds in the Nave. The buzz was electric, everybody greeting each other with hugs and pats on the back. To my horror only a few of the lads knew how to tie a tie, so I began re-tying their ties with oxford knots. White gloves on. (The white gloves that were issued were cheap floppy things, on a visit back to England I went to any army surplus store and bought a few pairs of proper white ceremonial gloves.) Medals were dangling around our necks. Whether you are religious or not, you cannot help but feel a tingle at the build-up, the noise, and the pride. I was the first foreigner to be invited to take part in this very special occasion. What an honour.

It took nearly an hour to leave the church and get onto the street. The Lady of Sorrows swaying, dipping and dancing all the way. It was once said, before volunteering to carry and be involved in a Cofradia, check the size of the church doors, the bigger the doors the bigger the float!

Once the first corner had been negotiated the second shift of costaleros including myself peeled off and went in search of food and a drink. The voluntary displaced foreigners (ex-pats) were all pleased and surprised to see me in the procession and asked, "I didn't know you were catholic?"

"I'm not," I replied, "I'm just the right height for the job in hand."

After refuelling, ten o'clock soon came around. It was my turn to help. Once in position and the knock rang through the carrying beam, up she went straight and true to generous applause. I was on the middle pole at the back under the cloak, so nobody could see me! This would have to change. Next year I would manoeuvre another rookie into that position. The struggle up to the Ermita was all I expected and the ascent, trying to march slowly with leather soled shoes on and 80kg of valuable cargo on your shoulder was tricky to say the least, but now it was the home run back to the church, and it was approaching two o'clock in the morning. After getting back into the church and witnessing the scramble for the carnations it was time for a drink. The problem was all my foreign mates had long since retired to bed. More integration, what a night.

Over the proceeding years the event has become more and more popular, with thousands more attending the celebrations, and many memories stick in my head. One year the route took a small diversion so we could stop outside the house of an old lady witnessing possibly her last Cristo. If one of our group passed away then a black ribbon was tied to one of the lamps. Hip flasks became visible during the frequent rests. One year the weather was threatening rain. The evening had remained dry until a couple of hundred metres from the church. Juan's phone rang and he relayed the message, the military band in front of us parted like the Sea of Galilee and off we went in double time reaching the sanctuary of the church just before the heavens opened. On enquiring who phoned him, he said, "Granada airport, radar." Even in these provincial backwaters we have the use of technology.

My assistance in carrying has somewhat diminished as of late, not just because of my bad leg but the young lads joining the Brotherhood are a little bit taller than me, so the cross beams are way above my shoulder. Being part of the Cofradia and trained to carry the load, I have also helped carry Saint Sebastian on January 20th, Saint Mark on April 23rd and Santa Filomena on August 8th.

Olives
Milkers, Whackers, Ticklers, Vibrators

YOUR VERY FIRST TASTE OF THE oil you have produced will stay with you like your very first kiss. Having been involved in agriculture in the UK I might have guessed that gathering and producing would not have let me go. Before moving to Spain, I thought olives appeared at the bottom of a Martini glass or stuffed with red pepper or anchovy. Olive oil was something that was kept in the medicine cabinet, heated and poured into one's ear on complaint of earache to mother.

The property we bought had six olive trees. Great high things that provided lovely shade.

Until they began to ripen towards mid-November, I never took much notice, and then on Boxing Day a bough broke free, crashing down and narrowly missing one of our guests. The bough was so laden with fruit we thought we had better pick them rather than let them rot or feed the birds. Sixty kilos later we went to a very small private mill and received fifteen litres of our very own olive oil. Was it extra virgin? Was it virgin? Did we care? It was ours and it tasted like nothing on earth. Fresh, peppery, aromatic, creamy. We were hooked. Well I was, my daughter ran a mile when harvesting was mentioned, and the wife disappeared into the kitchen. Harvesting olives can be a mundane, tedious, back breaking chore, but the rewards far outweigh the sacrifice.

History is what has happened in the past, it may be recent, or it might be distant, olives go back so far it is hard to imagine the

Mediterranean basin without them. Around our town, Órgiva we have a path (sendero), where you can stroll for a good time passing olive trees that are ancient. Try to imagine who planted them and cared for them. Olive trees do not have birth certificates, so the age is difficult to predict. You cannot count the rings like a normal tree. But now with carbon dating some trees are reputed to be 4,000 years old. Bethlehem has a very old one reputed to be 7,000 years old. They are a vine-type tree with new growth creeping up the external girth of the trunk, making them look like bent, stooped old men. Often the main trunk is hollow, allowing sanctuary for all, even the campesino's (peasant farmer) tools. The trees around Órgiva must be a thousand years plus. It's a pleasant walk that I recommend to all.

Olive leaves were found fossilised on the Aegean island of Santorini dated circa 37,000 years BC. They are still farmed there today. The Bible refers to olives at least 120 times and the trees at least 100 times.

Jesus was crucified on an olive wood cross. The Romans used olive oil like the Greeks today, 23kg was the minimum estimated consumption per person per year. The Greeks consume the most in modern times 22kg per person per year.

The olive is akin to the grape in the Mediterranean. But which one would you choose as a family favourite? One will give you warmth, light, cooking, massage, flavour, the other, well? It's a difficult choice. I like both. With over 700 cultivated varieties worldwide spanning six continents the Olea Europaea has brought wealth, trade, corruption, war-disputes and a lot of pleasure to millions for thousands of years, and will continue to do so, because when you get involved in oil production it is like a drug, it's addictive.

There are roughly 800 million olive trees spread over the world. China has 20 million, 90 % are around the Mediterranean and Spain has more trees than any other country. But Italy sells more olive oil than anybody else. (Overheard in a New York deli: "Which oil shall I buy? Buy what the Italians buy. What, Spanish?")

The industry has an annual global turnover of over E10 billion and two million metric tonnes of oil are consumed worldwide every year.

The Olea Europaea is a member of flowering plants such as Jasmine, Lilac and the Ashes. It is classified as a fruit, so olive oil is essentially a fruit juice.

European subsidies are still paid to olive farmers, and they normally get their cut in November for the previous harvest. In the past the subsidies have been abused. Firstly, farmers were paid on the number of trees they owned, so the root balls were covered with soil, and as if by magic one tree became three. Then the EU moved the goal posts on the weight produced, so big fat varieties were planted, no good for oil but water weighs well. There's an old saying, 'If there is a hole in the fence it will be found, take the fence down'.

Farmers all around the world have always found marketing their wares difficult. Just look at the UK, we had the Milk Marketing Board, Potato Marketing Board, Wool Marketing Board and the Egg Marketing Council. All controlling the price and skimming the cream off the top, it's the supermarkets' turn now. The Spanish olive growers are no exception, they produce the most oil, but the Italians have cornered the American market.

When milk quotas were introduced, dairy farmers in the UK had been encouraged to produce as much high protein, high fat milk as possible, breeding plans go back generations to improve production, longevity, confirmation. Suddenly stop, change direction, it's a bit like turning around an oil tanker. But with quotas came an opportunity, an asset, an asset the farmers did not own the year before. Trading became normal, some farmers sold their new asset, mothballed the dairy and enjoyed a less stressful life. Quotas are now over, and a lot of old dairies are up and running again. It's that old fence again. It could be the same with cannabis, and even as I write, Canada is about to become the first country to legalise the use of the plant.

Spain has over 260 different varieties of olive trees in production, eaters as well as oil producers. Thirty-two million tonnes of eating olives were exported to the USA alone last year. Each region and province have their favourites for oil production and of course the climate and height above sea level has its say. Spain exports more eating olives than any other country, Morocco comes second.

The cartoon character Olive Oyl along with her brother Caster Oyl were created in 1919, before Mickey Mouse. The Spanish respect for olives meant they call Olive Oyl, Rosario!

The Moors influenced the Spanish crop with the introduction of better varieties grafted onto Roman root stock. In fact, the Spanish word for oil is aceite and for olives is ace tunas and both words originate from Arabic. Some very old trees sprout from the root ball the original stock, tiny little olives called acebuches. Named after a village not far from us. So small if you harvest them in good quantity tell the miller otherwise, they will fall through the screen and be wasted. They produce fantastic oil.

The most popular variety in Spain is the Picual. Most large producers vary their varieties to spread out the harvest, which could span five months, starting late November, but for smaller producers the start of the harvest is governed by the mill. If it's not open then don't start, the early December holidays 6th and 8th is the normal time for the hobby grower to get going. Most olive trees produce their biggest crop every other year. The ripening process is fascinating to watch, my olives go from green to purple to black. This inspired the Órgiva rugby shirt.

We had a bunch of mates arriving on their Harleys, all had connections with the rugby club back in England, and as tradition has it a tour shirt was requested. After they arrived exhausted from their ride, they requested to borrow my car so supplies could be purchased. They returned with a car full of beer. "We got the naughty stuff; look it's got 'sin' written on the tin." I had to inform them 'sin' means without. Without alcohol. Another trip to town was swiftly organised. So, a shirt was designed, green, purple and black hoops, resembling the ripening olive with the twin towers of the Órgiva church on the left breast and Bar Canada on the right as sponsors. We all looked like ball boys from Wimbledon.

The early variety, pre-Christmas in our area is the Martena producing a green peppery oil that gets the back of the throat. An Australian olive oil producer once said, "Mate, if I want chlorophyll, I'll suck a leaf."

Picuals are best harvested around Christmas and New Year time, when you get a higher percentage of extra virgin oil. The prediction of the new season can be seen as early as May, by the amount of blossom on the trees, and by October the olive fronds are bowing their heads as the weight of the impending crop increases. The longer you leave the harvest, the higher percentage return you get. But the longer you wait the more olives you lose onto the ground. I'm happy with a 20 to 22% return. By percentage return I mean 20 litres of oil per 100kg of olives. One of our neighbours waited until April and achieved 33%.

Olive trees are drought resistant, but they do like a good watering and some natural fertiliser; sheep droppings are good, but chicken manure is excellent. During the season take away all the suckers from the root base so the energy goes into the top of the tree and the fruit. Olives blossom in mid-May, laying down a carpet of tiny light-yellow flowers beneath the tree, also a fine white cobweb appears around the tiny new fruit. This is nothing to worry about, it is not a fungus just part of the blossom. Allergies are common during this time, watering eyes and runny noses.

During harvesting I like to prune; this makes picking easier. There is a Spanish saying 'God does not like olives so keep your trees low'. They respond well to pruning which encourages new growth and a better crop. 'Make me poor and I will make you rich'. Dense trees and crossed branches are no good, a swallow should be able to fly through the tree without hitting anything!

During April you can look down onto the valley of Órgiva and think it's the land of the long white cloud, bonfires are everywhere and it's the last chance for burning before the fire permissions run out. Looking down from a high road onto a recently pruned olive grove the old trees look like giants with their heads chopped off.

After risking life and limb climbing and pruning, I decided to purchase a chainsaw on a pole. With the extensions in the machine I can cut safely from the ground up to five metres. Get it right and there's no sawdust in your eyes either. The heads are inter-changeable, so this year a tickler was purchased for harvesting. As men get older their toys get more expensive! Glory days. Don't forget ripe olives are easier to harvest than ones that are not ready.

Olive logs are considered the best locally for burning and are not cheap. Even in southern Spain we get cold winters.

We were living in one of the guesthouses and needed more logs for us and the visitors. Asking Juan, a Spanish friend about where I could buy some logs (leña) he gave it some thought and told me Adolfo has some.

So, we arranged to meet Saturday morning, after the obligatory coffee and a top up of brandy (it was a bit chilly) we set off to look at the logs. Well what confronted me was a mountain of olive wood. "I only want a tonne," I explained in my poor Spanish. Adolfo shrugged his shoulders and said you take it all or the man from Granada will buy it. Juan pulled me to one side and explained the price was very good and as I owned a chainsaw and a trailer to deliver with, I could process the wood into sensible sizes and resell the firewood, covering my costs and keeping warm for nothing.

A deal was struck. Well, on returning home (after another pit stop in the bar) Sarah asked did I manage to get some wood? I confirmed I had bought some and it was being delivered next Saturday.

The day arrived, and after the obligatory visit to the bar, two lorries and a JCB turned up at Adolfo's, loading began, then off we went to the weigh bridge (bascule de Puente), and nine lorry loads later, 49 tonnes of logs littered our land. Sarah came back from Motril and her jaw hit the floor. "Welcome to the log business," I exclaimed enthusiastically. Juan was right, it did keep me warm, splitting and cutting logs is like going to the gym every day.

After selling the initial 50 tonnes so quickly I was on the hunt for more supplies. Our bank manager, Pablo, came from Jaen, the centre of olive production. I asked him if he knew anybody who sold firewood in bulk at competitive prices. "Yes," he said. The price was so good I asked him if he could organise the delivery of two articulated lorry loads. He would guarantee my credit and they could deliver next week. It's always wise to buy out of season as the price per kilo is low. The day came and as the lorries trundled into the delivery area and tipped, I realised why the price was so good. It was all olive root. Olive root burns very well and very hot, but processing it is hard work. Another lesson learnt.

Large estates run a programme of re-planting trees every eighty years; this is about the life of a productive olive tree. During 2010 when the olive prices were low many local farmers were eyeing their old trees as cash, cutting the old trees down and selling the wood. Some even got permission to dig them up for transplanting, and sold them to people that wanted instant ornate gardens. They do transplant well, but it must be like selling your children.

Diseases and parasites are a continual problem with olive trees, while trying to keep the crop as organic as possible. The olive fly (Dacus Oleae) can produce three to six generations a year. One female can lay between 50 and 400 eggs in its life span which lasts six to eight months. The fly measures about 5mm in length, is reddish brown in colour, has large red eyes, small antennae and clear wings. The larvae are yellowish, white maggots with a pointed head.

They lay the eggs on the fruit and then the larvae burrow into the fruit emerging as a fly. They can over winter in fallen fruit.

Fly traps are the best way to control them in the nicest way. Plastic bottles with holes in the tops hung in the branches with a solution of ammonium salts 4% solution or try torula yeast, three to four tablets per litre of water. Maggot infected fruit can cause bad tasting-oil, and a good windy November tends to be nature's way of blowing off the damaged berries. We used to have crop spraying planes fly over and douse all and sundry whether you wanted it or not. Some growers would put out a white cross made of sheets to say, 'no thank you'.

After pruning it is important to dispose of the cuttings either by burning or feeding them to the local goats. The larger branches should be logged up and covered as the fly population will evacuate the cut material and possibly move on to its next target. You will notice a fine powder on the wood a couple of weeks after pruning. This was discovered by a friend in Devon. I managed to get some freshly cut chunky olive logs back to their farm for decoration in the inglenook fire place when not in use. After a couple of weeks, I got a phone call from them. "The house is full of flies we can't identify, and they seem to be coming from those logs you gave us." I assured them they were harmless, and the temperature would kill them off. Whoops.

Diplodia Canker is a fungus that causes ugly nodules to form on the branches, it can stop the development of the tree and needs pruning out. The dust found on the cut branches of olive wood is caused by the escaping Olive Bark Beetle, a real pest in some parts of the olive producing world.

In southern Italy they are fighting a new threat called Xylella Fastidiosa. Large areas of ancient olive groves are being wiped out with this pathogen. It's a bacterium that inhibits the movement of water and nutrients in the tree. The bacteria are spread by the spittlebug secreting saliva and is known as a hitch-hiking pest. Further research in Italy has had success in fighting the problem by making the trees stronger, cleaning the trees of dead or dry wood, treating with copper sulphate, iron sulphate and liberal fertiliser in the form of cow dung. The attacks seem to be on neglected trees so by using natural remedies this makes the trees stronger and more likely to be able to fight the infection. Some strong trees may recover but it's a progressive illness that can take up to three years to kill the trees.

Remember what happened to the Ash trees, Olive is related to that species.

Harvesting olives can be done in many ways. Many newcomers to the task dream up all manner of ways of getting the berries off the trees. The large estates use vibrators on the front of tractors, that grip the trunk, unravel a large upside-down umbrella and shake, this is then deposited into a trailer, but you need a lot of uniform trees to warrant this kind of investment.

In some areas I have noticed olive trees being planted very close together in tight rows shaped like cones, again this is for mechanical harvesting. These estates have their own mills and can get the picked fruit processed within hours of harvest, an ideal scenario. Any olives that end up on the floor are swept up with blowers and processed in a different way. On a well-run estate nothing is wasted.

In Croatia olive mills are few and far between, harvested olives are preserved in nets in the sea until sufficient have been collected to make the journey to the mill worthwhile.

Some local Spanish growers don't have transport to take their olives to the mill so once a week a lorry does the rounds collecting sacks of olives. Each sack is weighed by a weigh bar, a hook is inserted into the sack and lifted by two people and the weight is read and recorded.

Smaller producers rely on co-operatives. Our local guys will harvest every day and take their gatherings to the mill that day or every other day, in sacks, crates or loose in a trailer. They will be cleaned, weighed and a ticket produced as a receipt. You can tell by the queues of vans, pick-ups and other modes of transport waiting till late in the evening to get their day's toil weighed, who are the popular millers.

This harvesting can use the whacking method. Bamboo poles, cut years before so they are dry and weigh less, are used with nets lying on the land that is weed free and rolled flat. You then beat the hell out of your beloved olive tree, breaking off all that new wood and shoots. A lot of your neighbours will benefit from this method as olives fly in all directions and can travel many metres. The nets are then picked up and along with the precious fruit, which is now bruised and deteriorating you have twigs, leaves, birds' nests, plastic bottles from fly traps and anything else that was caught up in the tree. Just remember olives are easier to harvest when ripe. Early harvesting can severely damage your trees, just remember the leaves transform the sunlight into energy and absorb carbon dioxide which turns into oxygen. Taoist Masters believe trees give off great healing properties as well as the product they produce, so please don't give your trees grief.

Having extracted all the debris from your nets, the olives are carefully poured into sacks. They are as slippery as fish and can make a run for it at any opportune moment. Now the olives in the bottom of the sack are beginning to get pressed before they have got to the mill, all that lovely oil getting absorbed into the hessian. You might have guessed I'm not an advocate of whacking (at least not olives).

Olive oil is a food, so in my opinion this fruit needs to be harvested with care and attention to detail. The growers who want their own oil back tend to be milkers. Again, good ground preparation is required, nets are placed around the tree and small plastic rakes are used to separate the fruit from the tendrils. Ladders, and sometimes tower scaffold (this made the neighbours chuckle) have been used to collect in safety. Picking while balancing on a rickety ladder risking life and limb to get the last olive is not wise or clever.

As soon as the berries are picked the acidity starts to rise, so it is important to complete a harvest as soon as possible. Acidity (as % oleic acid) is the most fundamental measurement of olive oil purity and freshness. The quality of olive oil is directly related to the degree of breakdown of the fatty acids in the oil. As the bound fatty acids break down, free fatty acids are formed, increasing the percentage of acidity in the oil. Acidity is a measure of the free fatty acids present in the oil and is directly related to its purity.

The quality of olive oil can be adversely affected during either maturation or by environmental conditions. Mishandling, processing and bruising during harvest can also contribute to a breakdown of fatty acids. Extra virgin olive oil is determined by acidity, below one percent is required according to the CEE 2568/91 regulation. A low acidity value also indicates a natural extraction process occurred soon after harvesting.

Getting a good harvesting team around you is important. The days start around 9am and providing a good lunch is essential, porkchops and baked potatoes cooked in the embers of the olive pruning's get the taste buds going. The day ends around 6pm with ample supplies of beer. I aim for a three-day harvest and store the picked olives in crates or loose in the trailer in a dark place if possible. A pre-booked slot in your favourite mill is essential.

Ticklers are new a generation of harvesters, long poles with oscillating fingers driven by a car battery or a two-stroke engine. They cost around E600 but once you have operated one, bamboo poles are out. Nets are spread around the tree and with two people to move them you are away; with a good crop you can harvest a tonne a day. The fruit is not damaged, and the trees stay intact.

A Spanish friend, Juan Canada, who has a lot of trees, does not use nets. He prepares the ground well, tickles with his machine, then his wife with a back-pack blower blows them into heaps and his 82-year-old mother-in-law shovels them into crates which go on to the link box of the tractor, then into the tipping trailer and off to the mill. This season he harvested 24 tonnes. At 75 cents a kilo that's not bad going! Angles, Juan's wife, told me the women could collect 50kg a day on their hands and knees.

Taking olives to the mill is a gratifying experience, but how do you choose which mill? The Spanish have a saying, 'every miller will rip you off, it depends on the one you like the best to let him rip you off'. We have one miller in Órgiva whose name is eleven eggs (once huevos). I wonder why! It's almost like end-of-term excitement. Everybody estimates how many kilos you have, and other farmers take a quick glance at your crop, but the foreigners' (guiris) crops are always cleaner than the locals, because the locals know the twigs and leaves will be blown out before weighing.

So, it's your turn, once you have given your information to the miller, this should be on the certificate of transport you have with you. If you get stopped by the Guardia Civil on the way to the mill and you have no proof of where your harvest has come from then they could impound your hard work and fresh olives.

The olives are poured into the first hopper, then they travel up a conveyer belt to a vibrating sieve to clean the earth or stones away, then a blower, like a winnower, blows all the leaves into a separate container. This will be collected by the local shepherd (pastor) for his goats and sheep to eat.

Next, they travel to a weigh cell to be weighed, and in the office will be a digital display informing you of your efforts. With a receipt of the weight of your olives in your hand, it's now over to the process.

The olives are ground into a paste using tepid water, the mash is then spun in a centrifuge so the oil separates from the pulp and the vegetation water. This takes about two hours. The centrifuge will rotate at 3,000 rpm to separate the pulp from the mash and then at 6,000 rpm to separate the oil from the water.

The centrifuge has changed the perception of taste and quality of olive oil as the process can be carried out in a food grade environment. Mills will normally do a private pressing for a minimum of 500kg of fruit. You then decide on what size containers you want, sit on a stool and decant your fresh fruit juice(oil). As your containers mount up you are doing mental arithmetic on what percentage return you have achieved. As I said 20 to 22% is about right for Christmas time harvest. Buying olive oil is like going to the doctor. You must have faith in whom you are buying from. This way, having your own olives takes that doubt away. Another advantage of harvesting this time of year is unsuspecting guests and visiting relatives can join in the fun. We don't get many visitors that time of year anymore!

The attention to detail has paid off. Watering from snow melt off the mountains, minimum chemical use, natural fertilizers, olive fly control, the varieties of olives on your farm (finca), rapid harvesting and a good clean mill for processing will all help with your nectar. The vast majority of us will never taste the vintage wines of the world, nor will many ordinary people like us taste olive oil direct from the mill produced by ourselves.

The life of an olive mill owner must be interesting, they only work for a few months a year. Milling the olives is only part of their job, running a co-operative requires a huge amount of paperwork, the machinery needs maintaining, updates require installing, they have to find a market for the oil, have seminars to attend and they all have land to farm and look after. The most local olive mill to us had a reputation that was not the best. It was slow, allowed dirty olives into the process, and used old machinery. Granny was in charge and no investment was permitted. Disaster struck; a water store had been seeping into a supporting wall next to granny's bedroom. The whole lot collapsed killing the old woman in her bed. After a period of mourning the mill was rebuilt and the most modern Italian machinery installed. It is now the mill to go to. Very busy and the grandsons do an excellent job, but always remember their abuela (grandmother).

Now you must store your gold. A dark, cool space is needed, some will decant into glass, but the plastic containers the mill provides are fine. Just remember you cannot make good oil from bad olives. Olive oil does not improve with age, unlike wine. Wealthy estates who produce both lay down wine for new births, 400 bottles for boys and 100 for girls. Not so with olive oil.

Single variety oils are difficult to harvest as some root stock have more or one variety grafted onto them so the flavour of oil changes from year to year, but the multi-national olive oil companies blend oils, so their product is as standard as possible.

The oil you have ended up with is yours. You can't change it. Enjoy it. Not many people achieve what you have done. Trying to market your olive oil is a challenge many small producers dream of, but unless you can transport your product cheaply and have a market waiting for you back in northern Europe, then don't bother. I have taken olive oil back to the UK and given away samples to delicatessens who all agree it's a wonderful thing, but price, profit and supply provide a hurdle too high to jump. The EU raised the bar by banning olive oil to be decanted from large containers in shops to customers' own bottles. They even banned bars and restaurants from supplying their own oil, it had to be served at the table from sealed containers bought from an accredited supplier. That's not good when the restauranteur has his own olive grove. Next it will be orange juice!

Once your olives have been pressed the waste product is shipped off to a processing plant where more oil is extracted, lower quality and then what is left is dried and made into pellets and used as bio fuel. Nothing is wasted from this wonderful tree.

The traditional way of pressing olives used a stack system. The olives would be weighed and cleaned the same way, crushed into a pulp but then spread onto a circular mat called a capacha made of esparto grass. This would resemble a cowpat, in size and colour. The mat has a hole in the middle and fits over a steel pole, another mat is placed on top and so on until you have a stack maybe three metres high, looking like a massive doner kebab; oil is already percolating out of the bottom mats as the weight increases. This is collected into tanks below the stack. The stack is then moved to the press on a carriage. Pressure is then exerted from the floor at 400 atmospheres, nearly 6,000 psi.

After a couple of hours, the pressing would be complete, the stack dismantled, the mats cleaned of the pulp and the process starts again. A lot of farmers say because the mats can't be cleaned properly the olives you put in the top of the stack someone else will get the oil. The oil is then put through a slow centrifuge to separate the water.

I used to take my olives to a village called Otivar, a good hour's drive away. Setting off at 6am to be sure to be first in line, but somebody always beat me. Now this mill was more like a club, taking your food with you, you could expect to be there for a good many hours. With a raging fire to cook on and a fine selection of local wines to sample the time seemed to slip by. Along with a sneaky 40 winks. Siestas are for after lunch. Returning to Órgiva some eight hours later with my prized product and proudly going to the local bar for the Spanish to sample. Some people ask for trouble.

On one such outing, a group of friends wanted to see the olive mill in action. I went early as normal and the rest of the group was to follow at a more sociable hour. As it was a Sunday a table was booked at a very popular restaurant nicknamed the Chicken Shack in the village of Otivar, overlooking the mill itself.

After a guided tour of the process and as my oil was not ready, we retired for lunch. The restaurant's speciality was whole chickens stuffed with apple. Very nice. I had a call that my oil was ready for decanting so off down the precarious road to the mill. The date was 12/12/2010, 904kg of olives, 180 litres of oil, this was an early harvest for me, but a 20% return at a pressing cost of 130 euros including the containers.

Back up the hill with my precious cargo, the other cars were loaded with replete happy people, so off we set for Órgiva. About six kilometres out of Otivar my mobile rang with a rather distraught Sarah on the other end. "You bastard, you left me behind." I thought she had got into another car, how was I to know she was still in the toilet powdering her nose? So, having completed a rapid two-point turn with the trailer on behind, I retrieved the distraught woman. I think the reaction goes back to the day she was adopted. It's not nice being left behind.

Tasting olive oil and trying to decipher the nuances of the essential fruit juice can be a complicated business. The colour does not normally affect the tasting, samples are tasted in tinted glass bowls like a brandy glass without the stem, and a cover to capture the aroma. Fruit enzymes give the oil aroma and taste.

First of all, the style is discussed, is it: aggressive, assertive, pungent, bitter, delicate, gentle, fresh, fruity, green, harmonious, balanced, rustic, earthy, spicy, strong or sweet?

Next the aromas and flavours: apple, banana, lychee, melon, pear, ripe olive, tomato, eucalyptus, grass, flower, green leaf, hay, mint, herb, violet, avocado, almond, walnut or chocolate.

The defects of an oil are a little bit simpler, rancid means oil that has been exposed to air, soapy, fatty, greasy, flat, earthy (dirty olives) or fly. Olive oil will take on flavours if stored near other products; garlic and onions can be culprits. Be aware. But the question has to be asked, how was olive oil discovered? If you pluck an olive straight from the tree and eat it you will spit it out, it's so bitter. If you squeeze a ripe olive the juice is not very oily and tastes horrible, like most natural products discovered back in the Dark Ages, it makes you wonder. How?

The health benefits of extra virgin olive oil are well documented, this helps in marketing. An oil sold in Greece is packaged well and comes with a flyer. A biblical quote, three recipes and grandmother's secrets, olive oil folk lore remedies, olive oil will cure frizzy hair, constipation, insect stings, burns, baldness, bad nails and scuffed furniture.

An elderly French woman attributed her longevity to olive oil. She had reached the age of 102 and said, "I take a swig of olive oil every day and I have only one wrinkle and I'm sitting on it!"

Extra virgin olive oil is rich in mono-unsaturated fats, about 24% of the oil is saturated fats with omega-six and omega-three fatty acids. But with 73% fatty acid, mono-unsaturated fat called oleic acid is very healthy. Mono-unsaturated fats in extra virgin olive oil are also heat resistant making it a good choice for cooking with.

Extra virgin olive oil is loaded with powerful antioxidants, these antioxidants are biologically active and may help fight serious diseases. This includes antioxidants that can fight inflammation and help prevent the cholesterol in our blood from becoming oxidized, both crucial steps in the heart disease process. Inflammation is thought to be among the leading drivers of many diseases, including cancer, cardiovascular disease, metabolic disorders, diabetes, Alzheimer's, arthritis and obesity. The antioxidants in extra virgin olive oil can reduce inflammation which is one of the main reasons for its health benefits. Olecanthal is shown to work in the same way as Ibuprofen.

The relationship between extra virgin olive oil and strokes has been studied extensively. A total of 841,000 subjects were studied and the only source of mono-unsaturated fats associated with a reduced risk of stroke and heart disease was extra virgin olive oil.

Heart disease is the most common cause of death in the world, so the Mediterranean diet led to extensive research on the inclusion of extra virgin olive oil in daily consumption. It lowers inflammation, protects LDL cholesterol from oxidization, improves the function of the lining of the blood vessels, and may also prevent unwanted blood clotting. It has also been shown to lower blood pressure.

Eating fat does not make you fat nor does consuming large amounts of olive oil.

Having lived in southern Spain for nearly two decades the Mediterranean diet confuses me. Restaurants rarely serve fresh vegetables, at the market, stalls are full of fruit and vegetables, in a time when smoking is proven to be dangerous to health our town opens a second tobacconists and alcohol is consumed on a steady daily basis. Is this truly the Mediterranean diet? This olive oil stuff must be extremely powerful to overcome such abuse.

Olive oil is now appearing in cocktails. Connoisseurs of cocktails enjoy the martini with the olive but now the oil is being added to achieve mouthfeel and extra virgin olive oil can be a major force in giving the cocktail this texture. Fat washing was achieved by using animal fats, but extra virgin olive oil has now taken over. The Oliveto cocktail was invented by Pip Hansen in the Marvel Bar, Minneapolis. It consists of gin, lemon juice, syrup, Liquor 43, egg white, extra virgin olive oil and ice. It has a silky meringue texture, and an emulsified sour taste. The egg white after fighting the opposing forces of the fat, produces a lovely foam and it's great to witness people's reaction on their first sip. Liquid chap stick!

Extra virgin olive oil appears to be highly protective against diabetes. Olive oil has beneficial effects on blood sugar and insulin sensitivity. The antioxidants in olive oil can reduce oxidative damage due to free radicals, which is believed to be one of the leading drivers of cancer.

This reminds me of another super product I used to supply called Colostrum. I say supply as selling it was no problem. It was based on Bovine colostrum collected from cows in their third lactation and freeze dried (after the calf had its fill). Nature's miracle. It contained proteins, carbohydrates, vitamins, minerals and antibodies. It would be used by shepherds, stockmen, even horse breeders. It was also supplied in capsules for human consumption as it boosted the white corpuscles which fight infection.

We now own a lot more trees and harvest other people's, to keep the annual harvested amount around the 1000kg mark producing 200 litres of oil. Extra virgin olive oil is the only type that contains all the antioxidants and bioactive compounds that you need. To guarantee this quality buy some land with olive trees on or get friendly with someone who has.

May Crosses

THE MAY CROSSES FESTIVAL CELEBRATED ALL over Andalucia has an amazing history. The true cross was found by St Helena. Her son Constantine, who became emperor in 306AD, had a dream the night before a battle that if he held a cross in the sky before the conflict and uttered the words, 'in hoc signo vinces', (by this sign you shall conquer), he would be victorious. The next day as his enemies were crossing a bridge ready for battle, it collapsed, and the war was won. As a pagan this did not convert him to Christianity, but he did legalise it. His mother took to the Faith with a passion. When Helena was aged 85, she had a vision of her own which led her to the long-lost True Cross on which Christ died. She led the archaeologists to the site where priceless relics were uncovered, Holy nails, the True Cross and the seamless robe. The story of the Robe was made into a film called The Robe, the first film in Cinemascope.

The decorated crosses originated in its modern-day format in Cordoba in 1954. A competition was launched by the town hall (ayuntamiento). Local barrios and Brotherhoods (hermandades) created crosses covered in flowers and surrounded with memorabilia from the past. Old sewing machines, ancient pots and pans. Quite often an apple with a pair of scissors with just one blade stuck into it. In Andalucia an apple is called a manzana, also a pero, the word for but in Spanish is pero. They are saying, 'don't be negative, cut out the but in your life, be positive! It's the start of May'. These celebrations take place at the beginning of May over the first weekend. Bars are often set up near the cross so you can enjoy a glass while admiring the handiwork. Towns will create a map of the competitors so you can visit them all. This year in Órgiva there are 18 to visit. They normally have a rural theme with the girls wearing their flamenco dresses and the men dressed in horse-riding garb with flat tweed caps. Mother's Day, immaculate conception, first Sunday in May.

Corpus Christi

CORPUS CHRISTI, THE BODY AND BLOOD of Christ, is a movable feast, celebrated on the Thursday after Trinity Sunday. Two months after Maundy Thursday. The Eucharist celebrated the day before Good Friday was always a sombre affair as it was during Lent. Juliana of Liege dedicated her life to recognise the body and blood of Christ to be celebrated properly so Corpus Christi came to be around the mid 1200's. After holy mass on the Thursday of Corpus a procession takes place with the monstrance held aloft.

Granada is the nearest city to celebrate Corpus Christi, and the place shuts down for a week. Avoid Granada during this week if you need anything important. A massive area is converted to an elaborate fairground, with stalls selling everything you could imagine and private marquees hosting week-long parties. The bull ring is in full use with famous matadors visiting. The type of bull fighting during this week is the standard but on one day Rejoneos are fought, bull fighting just on horseback. There is a procession on the Wednesday called the Tarasca, this is a mannequin dressed up in the latest fashion that will influence what the girls will wear in the future. Thursday sees the procession of the Monstrance. The procession on the Sunday is called the Octave of the Corpus. Órgiva has a parade, 6.30pm on the Sunday after mass.

In a town near Burgos, Sasamon they have a tradition called Baby Jumping. New-born infants are placed on mattresses on the street and men dressed as the devil jump over them holding whips and very large castanets. Strange but true.

Easter Uprisings

THE HEAP OF RIVER STONES THAT was once the small farmhouse were carefully stacked in piles; most still had the whitewash on one of its sides. This material would come in handy when we stone clad the new farmhouse. With careful thought and lots of sketches Sarah and myself came up with a design and plan for our new house, taking into consideration the temperature variations of the seasons, and the sun height in winter and summer. This can keep the harsh summer sun off your windows when the sun is high and let the winter sun shine in when the sun is lower. Flood irrigation has got to be brought into the equation when planning a build. You don't want the acequia water flooding into your property or undermining the foundation. We decided phase one would be the kitchen, diner, lounge in one space and the office, laundry and store with a shower room and toilet in the other space. The bedrooms would come later, we could sleep in the caravan. Drainage of sewage and grey water is high on the list. Most country houses in this part of Spain have what they call a black hole as a septic tank (pozo negro). It's a large tank built with concrete blocks in a honeycomb structure. This allows the liquid to drain while the solids remain trapped inside the tank. Evidence of such old tanks is hard to find as no breather pipes are visible or inspection covers, but rest assured they will be close, sometimes beneath the actual house. They never seem in need of being emptied. The more up-to-date septic tanks have a three-chamber filtration system with a stone filled soakaway on the outlet. Always put a breather pipe in the run as this will allow the waste to flow with equal pressure. This is what we decided to build; you can buy them now ready formed in fibreglass. The grey water was planned to irrigate the olive and almond trees.

Next was the oversight, the floor and foundations of the proposed building. In my opinion the most important part of the whole structure, get this right and the rest should be easier. On a traditional flat roof design, the new concrete roof beams are seventy centimetres to the centres. Make your footprint of the house so the roof beams fit. Much easier when you come to put the roof on!

We got a digger in to dig the foundations and the trench for the waste pipes. The land being in the old river bed meant we could come across some very large boulders and we did. Massive things that must have come down with the glacial flow. These massive stones often make up the corner stone of many buildings in the area. Going around them was the only option. Dynamite was the other! With the metal cages in the foundation trenches and the copper earth wire in place it was time to mix and pour the concrete. The hobby mixer we had bought was not man enough, so a new shinny 150-litre machine was bought much to my delight.

With the foundations poured (the Spanish way is to build off a raft of concrete) next was the floor. Using a block which is twenty centimetres high we created the pond. In here went the membrane, the insulation, the necessary waste pipes and the weld mesh. Next the concrete floor was laid for a nice level finish ready for the walls to be constructed. I employed a Spanish labourer, as I thought it would be useful to pick up some of the language. Manolo was a great strapping lad. I knew he had a speech impediment, but I didn't realise he was partially deaf as well. So much for learning more Spanish, the union didn't last long.

Juan appeared on the Tuesday, and said, "Are you ready to build the house?"

"I think so," I replied. We calculated the number of thermal blocks required (tonto blocks) windows, doors, lintels, sand, cement, roof beams, roof blocks and steel bar. "What about the DPC (damp proof course)?" I enquired.

"The what?" Juan replied. I explained the theory to Juan, so a roll of asphalt was added to the shopping list to be cut into strips and used as the DPC. The build was to take place over the weekend. All the products were delivered on the Wednesday morning, and my team and Juan's team were employed to start prompt at 8.00am on Saturday morning. Easter Saturday. I was concerned that the permission had not arrived, but Juan assured me this would not be a problem, as it was Easter nobody is around all weekend. With several barrels filled with water and electricity supplied by our neighbour, the construction started. It was difficult to persuade the Spanish team about the DPC, they were afraid the house might slip off!

By Sunday lunchtime 600-odd blocks had been laid and the ring beam was in place, an Easter uprising had taken place!

The roof went on Monday and the concrete on the Tuesday. The roof, complying with local tradition, is flat. Concrete beams, which resemble the cross-section of a railway track, are placed on the completed walls and blocks are placed in between them. These can be concrete (traditional) or now polystyrene. At twenty-five centimetres thick (or thicker) this provides great insulation for both winter and summer. The roof is supported by a forest of acrow props to carry the weight of the impending concrete. A neighbour who had a finca down the lane and who worked in the town hall nearly fell off his bike when he had seen what we had achieved in such a short time. On his next trip down the lane he stopped and told us our permission was ready to be collected from the town hall. This was a relief. The system is as follows: submit your estimated cost and plans into the town hall, wait for a very long time, collect the approved paperwork from the town hall, go to the bank and pay the tax, back to the town hall get it all stamped and off you go. No site inspections, no building inspectors, just get on with it.

Easter was the start of our busy time down at the cottages and this Easter was no exception. With all three houses full, we had moved up to the building site and lived in the caravan. This was fine as the weather was kind and our neighbour allowed us to climb over the wall and use his unfinished casita for our ablutions. Alex thought it was great and loved the adventure. What she was upset about was the lack of Easter eggs. They don't do them in Spain. I think we made up for it with other types of confectionery.

Talking of Easter eggs many years ago back in England, Sarah donated an Easter egg plus other items for a charity draw at our local pub. During the draw I noticed an Easter egg that looked familiar. "Where did that prize come from?" I asked.

"Us," was the reply.

"Well we had better win it as I have mined the back as well as the smarties inside." I got a right old telling off.

By now we had experienced the transitions of the seasons, late summer, autumn, winter and spring. The seasons certainly give you different temperatures, with variations of baking hot summer days and warm airless nights, to chilly frosty winter mornings and days of continuous rain. Grateful when October arrives, the cooling fan can be switched off in the bedroom, showers can be taken slightly warmer and clothes can be adorned with pockets so documents, mobile phones and wallets don't need to be in the man bag that you always leave behind somewhere.

We can get 320 days of sunshine a year. This leads to problems when working outside, as you never seem to get a day off due to the weather being inclement! When packing to move to Spain don't throw away your winter woollies, you will need them. With snow on the Sierra Nevada and on the Contraviesa in the winter we exist in a valley bowl chilled by both sets of mountains. Continuous frosts one year for eight weeks meant we had frozen oranges hanging on our trees. Spring arrives early in the Alpujarras, and the almond blossom soon arrives after Christmas in its varieties of whites, pinks and reds. The evenings pull out, so we still have light at 6.30pm, the mornings are still dark with lazy light at eight but still with a chill in the air. The broad beans are in flower in February as well as the yellow oxalis and violets which carpet the ground. Strong gusty winds can cause damage, and many summer parasols end up being destroyed as the winds pick up in the afternoons. September rain is not normal but when it arrives it leaves wisps of candy floss clouds clinging to the mountains' craggy outcrops. Rainfall is measured by the number of millimetres per square metre. So, beware before taking the leap, try to visit your chosen part of paradise as many times throughout the year to experience the seasons.

With the first layer of concrete on the roof, all handed up in buckets, it was time to let the concrete cure. Lashings of water are needed to let it set slowly. The slate surround was cemented in place. After this dry sand was heaved up and graded to give the roof the desired gradient so once the membrane was on, the rain would find its way to the spouts. That was the theory. It sort of worked. The membrane we used was asphalt, metre wide rolls that needed welding together with a blow torch. A very tricky operation. This I will never use again. Having demolished a few properties with this product on the roof you soon realise how brittle it becomes and does not move with the fluctuating temperatures we get. Thus, it cracks and lets in water after a few years and you never know where the leak is. As mentioned before EPDM membrane is the way forward.

It was interesting to witness the breakfast arrangements of the Spanish builders during our initial build. Starting work promptly at eight, they were never late. They stopped at ten for breakfast. No fancy sandwiches here, egg and cress, coronation chicken, prawn mayonnaise, no I don't think so. A white barra of bread, a tin of tuna or pate, chorizo or jamon, constructed in front of our very own eyes using granddad's penknife. The bread bara is as important to the Spanish as the croissant and baguette are to the French. This is washed down with a tin of beer, or a glug of wine from the bota (leather wine container). We offered coffee or tea but there were no takers. Three quick cigarettes from the packet, no rolling your own, wastes too much time and back to work at 10.30. They stopped for lunch at two and back on it at three. At the end of the day there was no time wasting to finish they just kept going until the cement ran out.

Safety on building sites is somewhat to be desired in our region, steel toe capped boots are rare, hard hats are even rarer and safety glasses are non-existent. Not on my building plot. Anybody who worked for us had to have the kit and use it. I supplied ample pairs of gloves and fashionable safety glasses (they would wear fashionable ones) for when operating angle grinders and other machinery that had one purpose in life and that was to throw what it could towards your face. Anyone found not using the glasses was invited to leave the site.

On a visit up to town once in May, the start of the tourist season and weekend communions, the council had decided to rip up the high street and replace it with cobbles and put a conduit under the road for the impending optic fibre internet supply. It was ten o'clock and breakfast time, the workers had their safety hats on, their fluorescent jackets on, and they were sat on pallets of cement enjoying their recently made barras and handing round bottles of beer!

An interesting observation is when the Spanish drink from a shared bottle the lips never touch the container. It's poured into the mouth, the same with the porron, the glass vessel for holding wine. It has the spout and you have to direct it into your mouth. Orson Welles refused to use one saying it reminded him of a bed bottle used in hospitals and demanded a proper glass. The porron was used when glass was expensive, and Ikea was not open and has become a symbol of Spanish dining as well as a popular tourist souvenir. It's the same with the pipote used for keeping drinking water cool in the summer often seen outside petrol station kiosks. It's poured into the mouth. The reason behind this is vaccinations or rather the lack of them. You did not want to catch some awful disease off your workmate. Inoculations and vaccines are now implemented all over Spain, but the habit still carries on because that's what your ancestors taught you.

The main structure of phase one of our new farmhouse was now up, that's the easy bit over and done with. Numerous planning meetings had to take place between Sarah and myself normally over a beer or two and tapas (free lunch) to decide on the positioning of sockets, lighting, outside lighting, kitchen style, wall and floor tiles, plaster finishes, ceiling beams and plumbing. The kitchen, a very important hub of the house was to be open-plan in the dining area. We were warned by some bar stool experts that normal kitchen units would not last five years as the carcloma beetle would eat anything wooden, and that brick pillars with tiled shelves and curtains was the answer. A tiled or granite work surface is much better than a Formica top. We opted for granite as Sarah had always wanted a granite work surface in her kitchen. Very expensive in the UK, natural sparkly black labradorite from South America was the choice and on receiving the quote from Jose there was no argument. The granite option works out much cheaper than tiles as the installation is so instant. Granite is easier to keep clean with no grout to get stained. The final bill for the granite was cheaper than the quote (would that happen in Blighty?). So, with some extra cash to splash we went for handmade local tiles in a Moorish pattern.

But also, not forgetting the guesthouses needed to be run, and the guests kept happy. On change over days it was always interesting to see what was left behind in the casitas, the normal was pasta, garlic, jam, tuna, a dribble of gin, alcohol free beer (bought by mistake), and old copies of the Guardian. We even found a couple of Viagra tablets once. Constant irrigation meant the plants and grass just kept on growing and thus needed cutting or pruning.

With first fix plumbing and electrics in place we decided we wanted smooth plastered walls; this took some doing as pink plaster does not exist in this part of the world.

Taking it easy and slowing down were now a distant memory. We found it important to make sure there was a definite transition between work and play. Having an endless supply of lemons helped! The weight was falling off the both of us and dieting a thing of the past. It does prove a point, if you burn more calories than you consume then that energy has to come from somewhere. Your reserves. As of writing this my reserves are back up to full capacity once more!

Receiving post and packages was a problem as the Spanish post delivery service does not deliver down unmade tracks. The post office had a few post office boxes for rent but not enough for the increasing population of our town. Eventually the post office moved to larger premises and a whole wall was dedicated to PO boxes. Plenty to go around, thirty-two euros for a year's rent. The post-delivery people use their own vehicles and security is lax. Often the postman would leave his trolley outside a bar to have a swift coffee and take an order from the barman for more broad beans that he grew. The post office began to get suspicious about more than one name using a box, so they declared that for every extra surname another thirty-two euros should be paid. When the Spanish have children, the child has the father's surname first and the mother's surname second. The wife retains her surname when she gets married. This would be easy to identify for the post office if the rest of Europe used this system. But we don't, so a Mr and Mrs Jones were getting billed twice and if a little Master Jones got a letter he would get billed as well. The solution was to organise a collection of private post boxes at the top of our road. A one-off cost, now the post office has many PO boxes for rent and no customers.

Packages are a little trickier, the rise in internet shopping has meant the courier service has improved no end. In the early day's packages were just dropped off at the petrol station. Even UPS sub-contracted, a promise they said they would never do. A friend's daughter needed some study books sent over from England so she could revise for some exams. They got lost and eventually turned up at the petrol station after she had gone home (none the wiser!). Our local bar is open six days a week, so we get our packages delivered there. The problem is not trying to check every day if it has arrived, even if you are not expecting anything!

Being a waiter in Spain is an important job, many are part of the family that own the bar or restaurant. They specialise in not having twenty-twenty vision, not noticing your glass is empty, instead chatting with their mates as you die of dehydration, or preferring to have a sneaky fag than collect dirty glasses and charging a little bit more just because you are a foreigner. They also roll up their sleeves when the bar needs decorating or reforming.

The tapas that accompanied your refreshment intrigued us; it was like a small advert of what you could have if you were really hungry. The bar staff would just shout to the kitchen the number of the assigned tapa and how many. I fear for the life of this free food as less and less bars provide it as a matter of course. It has an impact on restaurants trying to provide a proper menu. You go out for a meal in a restaurant, have a couple of drinks beforehand and then your appetite is diminished due to tapas.

All the waiters are experts at playing pool although you have never seen them actually play and they can build a wall better than you too.

Pepe, the co-owner of a very nice bar restaurant decided to clean the oven. After putting the strong cleaning fluid on the surfaces, he thought he would check it a couple of hours later. Not being able to see inside he got his lighter out, boom. Poor chap, all the hair on his arm was singed and his face glowed and glistened for a couple of weeks after.

We have over 30 bars and restaurants in town, and how they all make a living I don't know. Our own little joke about the food they serve goes like this. They go to the town hall and ask for the menu, the town hall ask, "What's the bar called?" and then print the menu. Meaning, they all serve the same local stuff! Pizza was on all the menus, but an Italian, Alberto opened a specialised pizza restaurant. We became good friends and Friday night was pizza night. On one occasion I had a pizza with asparagus on. The second mouthful of this delicious treat revealed something hard in my mouth. On inspection it was a piece of glass from the top of a bottle. Not wishing to draw the attention of the rest of the diners, I called Alberto over.

"Ah, that's where it went," was his reply. Italians!

We got taken out to lunch by an English neighbour after we had done him a few favours. When receiving the bill, Eric had forgotten his wallet (not unusual), so the waiter insisted that he should come back tomorrow and pay, but Eric went home, retrieved his wallet and came back and paid. He said the waiter was quite angry about this. Later that week I was talking to the waiter about this, I asked, "Why were you upset about Eric coming back to pay straight away?"

The waiter replied, "If he came back the next day, he might have had some more to drink!" Then we both agreed he was too tight to do that, with a chuckle. I have noticed bars offer a tab service to regulars.

Offices and shops don't have staff coffee-making facilities, they just go to the bar, get it there and take it back to work. It's not unusual to go to the bank at around ten in the morning and only find one member of staff on duty, it's coffee time. The siesta is still taken, mainly by shop and office staff. I have enough trouble waking up once a day not twice.

There are about nine different ways to take your coffee in Spain. The most common is café con leche, coffee with milk. Just ask if you want your milk hot or cool (calente, frio). Café Americano, just black coffee. Sugar or saccharine on the side. Leche manchada, hot milk with a few drops of coffee for that hint of flavour. Translated means stained milk. Café descafeinado. Decaffeinated coffee. The waiter will ask if you want it from the machine (de maquina) or packet (de sobre). It tastes just like the real thing. Café solo, strong, small and a kick like a mule, good for after a midday meal. Café cortado, small shot with hot frothy milk, takes away the bitterness of the solo. Café Bombon, condensed milk first and then a shot of espresso. Café con hielo, coffee with ice. You will get two cups, one with your coffee in it, and one with ice. Tip your coffee onto the ice, the ice cools the coffee. Very nice in the summer. The best is always last, carajillo. A shot of espresso and then your favourite liquor on top. Whiskey, rum, brandy or anise. Just to add to the choice you can take your coffee in a glass or a cup. A kilo of coffee beans costs the bar eleven euros, from this after grinding they can produce one-hundred and twenty cups of coffee. A popular bar can use up to nine kilos of coffee beans a week. I will let you do the sums!

Merienda is a tea-time snack for the children, between five and seven in the afternoon. It can be a long time from lunch, which is at two, to dinner that can be late, so the children need fortifying. In a bar I saw a grandma prepare a sandwich for her grandchild. She just pulled out of her magic bag all the ingredients she needed and made it then and there, without a murmur from the bar staff. The children come first.

The Spaniards' drinking routine is as follows. Glass sizes are important to note. Beer is normally served in two different sized glasses. A caña is a small glass with a stem, two-hundred mil, a tubo is what it sounds like, a tube containing three-hundred mil of liquid. Pints are rare but are appearing more and more, especially in tourist areas. I prefer bottled beer. These come in two different sizes, a quinto, which is a quarter of a litre and tersio, which is a third of a litre. I drink from bottles for two reasons, one is that it is always full, no froth (espuma) and two is that when I have the shakes, I don't spill it! Don't be surprised if the waiter picks up your glass when there is still some liquid in it, many locals don't empty their glass. Some say it's a drink for god, some say it's in case the King's peseta has been dropped into your vessel. I say they don't want to swallow the fly that has been swimming in their drink. If you hear a bell ring in the bar don't worry, they are not calling time, the bar will stay open as long as you are drinking, it's when a tip has been received, this is called propena. When visiting England, we frequent a wonderful pub in Great Torrington called the Black Horse. The locals are a great bunch who welcome you and let you enter into that great tradition, pub banter. This I can honestly say I miss.

A glass of wine is a copa, and a generous size as well. Spirits are dangerous as the amount dispensed is about the equivalent of quadruple in English terms. A single gin in the UK is more like homeopathy than a drink. Locally a spirit with a mixer is called a cuba libra. A good whiskey can be adulterated with a Coke chucked in with it.

I always take a good quality single malt with us to our Christmas Eve party with our Spanish friends. It has taken some years to persuade them to drink it neat or with water.

You don't seem to witness Spaniards on a drinking session, they are very measured in their routine, they drink a lot but in a steady way, not the binge drinking you see by us lot. On a visit to Jerez we stayed in a very nice hotel. As you may know Jerez is famous for its sherry, in fact if you want a sherry in a bar then ask for a Jerez or a Fino. We did notice that the mini bar in our room was devoid of anything local. Tio Pepe do a fantastic tour of their bodega (cellars).

The staff of the builders' merchants we use are quite often out in the bar after work having a cheeky one before going home, and they always buy me a beer on behalf of their boss. I wonder if they get an allowance for this generosity. You would not find that in England. Talking of builders' merchants and other businesses. Their postage costs must be negligible, I have never been sent a statement or a bill by post. They just wait until you come in to pay. Very trusting.

Small businesses like bars and small shops will close for holidays, they don't employ relief staff to keep the tills ringing, they just shut.

The no-smoking ban in public places which came into force the second of January 2011 was strange to observe. Before the total ban, if the bar was licensed for 60 customers, they had to have a segregated area for smokers. Small store rooms were built to reduce the square metres so smoking could take place as normal. Tobacco machines have remote switches to stop under age puffers buying their premature death, often these buttons were just left on top of the counter. When we arrived in the year 2000, supermarkets had ashtrays at the end of the aisles, and shoppers would light up and have a chat with their mates.

My daughter lived for a year in the ancient area in Granada called the Albaicen on a street called ashtray street (calle cenicero). The law stated that smoking was banned in an open terrace with four walls, within five hundred metres of hospitals, schools and plazas. Bars that had no outside terrace were affected but at least the kind weather let people who wanted to smoke could stand outside without catching pneumonia. This also meant the scroungers knew where to get a free cigarette and pick up fag butts for rolling their own. We still have a few bars that have totally ignored the law and allow smoking. On a visit back to England you can tell the pubs that are open by the congregation standing outside in the freezing rain killing themselves one way or another. Conversations can be interrupted when the person next to you just stands up and goes outside for a smoke. Very inconsiderate.

We have a lot of alternative living people here all free to do their own thing. Vegans, vegetarians, raw food believers treating their bodies like temples. What I can't understand is why do they all think their temples have chimneys. But like most European laws the Spanish pick out the best bits and disregard the rest.

The employment laws in Spain encourage employers not to employ each waiter for too long, otherwise their rights increase, so, it's quite normal to see the waiters doing a circuit of different bars, like on a rota. You sort of get the same feeling with supermarket staff. The bank managers we have met while we have been here have all been very friendly people, but as soon as you get to know them, they are transferred. It's the same with the town priest.

Órgiva has 6,000 residents. There is no fire station or fire brigade in town. Fire fighters are called Bomberos. The closest fire station is in Motril, forty minutes away. The Forestall (forest patrol and maintenance) have a huge four by four tender but it is no good for a town with narrow streets. After eighteen years we have just witnessed the first house fire in Órgiva for many decades.

Two fire engines roared up the high street one Friday evening, both looking lost. An Australian lady had fallen on her roof terrace and had broken her pelvis, and the Ambulance service could not bring her down the stairs as the stretcher would not navigate the tight corners of the stairwell. She was eventually recovered by being lowered over the side of the house mountain rescue style by the fire service. On another occasion the fire engine appeared to release a mechanic from a fatal accident, a lorry engine had fallen on his head.

We often get asked 'what do you like about living in Spain and what do you miss from living in the UK?'

The thing I like is the accountability of people, they all know each other. If a kid is caught doing something naughty, they know their parents will be informed very quickly, this in itself is a deterrent. The children will take granny out for a walk and not feel embarrassed in front of their mates. People shop every day, which means they talk to each other every day, and they buy fresh. No monthly shop to the hypermarket. To begin with we missed the variety of takeaway food options. I sometimes miss putting on a nice heavy overcoat during a cold winter's day, but we can always go up to the ski resort if we want to and play in the snow. We look at the snow every day during the winter while enjoying the warm sun. When you are working hard all day sometimes it's easier just to grab a takeaway curry or a pasty. We now have kebab, pizza, curry, wraps, even fish and chips if you know where to go!

Visitors ask us, "How often do you go home?"

Our reply, "Every night."

Refuse collection is a daily routine (except Sundays) here in Órgiva. The rubbish gets very smelly in the heat, so daily collection is necessary. Nothing like the UK, where it is once a fortnight I believe. Each householder has to take their refuse to the bins and the recycling. We have over 240 dumpsters scattered around the town and on its many roads to the surrounding hamlets, so there should be no excuse to see litter on the streets: half empty beer bottles, cigarette packets, broken plastic chairs, fizzy drink tins etc. All this detritus turns a beautiful town into a criticised dirty one. Street cleaners clear up the streets every day, some doing community service and some unemployed. They have a foreman who organises them, and while he is telling them where to go and which streets need cleaning, I have seen him unwrap his packet of twenty cigarettes and deposit the packaging on the pavement. Education and financial penalties must be the answer. We now have many waste bins on the main streets that are used mainly by visitors. Some local people drop litter and think it is job creation. We have our fair selection of bin divers, hippies and down and outs searching the bins for any tasty morsels. I'm only jealous because I'm too short to look inside! On a recent visit to France, I noticed they have locks on their dumpsters.

During recent heavy rain the dry barrancos can suddenly flood with a torrent of water that is life threatening, sweeping all before it in a tidal wave and cleansing a mountain of plastic drums, pipes, plastic sheeting, bottles, dead sheep and anything else that has just been chucked in the ditch, which is all swept out to sea. In Tablones we have a recycling centre, the Punto Limpio. It's a great place, no jobs worth council workers operating it, just friendly staff willing to help you dispose of your unwanted stuff. Now open on Saturday mornings but closed on bank holidays and fiestas.

Town councils can gauge the population of a town by the tonnage of garbage they dispose of. In Órgiva the amount of rubbish disposed of far outweighs the registered population. This can highlight the amount of unregistered people but also how many tourists visit the area. A strange but accurate barometer.

Owning a pet dog is a relatively new thing for the Spanish. They have dogs on the land and use them to hunt with and guard the premises, but to let them live in the house or flat is a strange phenomenon. They are generally known as mascots. To see a dog on a lead used to be unusual. If it's a hippy's dog then it might be on a bit of string. The problem comes when the lady of the house kicks the dog out in the morning along with the old man so she can do the cleaning and prepare the lunch. The old man has done his ablutions and wanders off for an early game of dominos, but the dog just goes and shits on the street. Things are improving and you do see dog mess being picked up and signs requesting such action. Poo bags are actually attached to leads in those little plastic tubes. There are now special bins with bags supplied installed in some of the streets in Órgiva. Stray dogs are being rounded up and the wonderful retired band of Brits (the Spanish think we are all retired) spend their time organising spay and neutering days kidnapping any unsuspecting four-legged furry animal with its breeding bits still intact. They have fund raising events and organise foster homes for dogs to be eventually adopted to their forever home. Some end up in Holland, Germany and the UK. The dogs that is!

In the campo it's nothing to hear packs of baying dogs communicating with each other for most of the night, and a hundred and one dalmatians comes to mind. This is great if you are a tourist and paid a small fortune to hire a farmhouse for a peaceful relaxing holiday or your child has school in the morning. When we went to Tenerife for a holiday, we barely heard a dog bark and asked a taxi driver about this subject.

He said, "It's illegal to let your dogs bark, we rely on tourism, and we want people to return, so it's in our own interest."

Veterinary practices are one-man bands and are used to dealing with big animal problems, so the advent of small animal work was a little bit different for them. One of our friends took their prized moggy in for a check-up. The cat escaped and was never seen again.

A shrug of the shoulders from Augustine the vet. "There are loads of cats around." In the UK because the vets are on call twenty-hours a day they form practices of several veterinary surgeons under one roof, so someone is always available. Not so here. We had now grown our dog collection to three: Maisie the original springer from Somerset and two of her offspring, Badger (Tejon in Spanish) and Curry. One weekend ten weeks before Christmas, both Maisie and Badger went off their feet, paralysed. Could I get hold of a vet? There was a veterinary conference in Seville, and they all seemed to be attending. We had to wait until the Monday until we could speak to somebody. It's a long time to wait when you have a problem like this.

I have a friend who is a vet in the UK and after some frantic phone calls we decided it was something they had ingested. When the local vet returned from his beany in Seville, blood samples were taken, and diagnosis turned out to be botulism. We reckon a dead chicken had been chucked into the barranco, the sun had baked the skin and the dogs had then had it for lunch. After ten weeks of constant care we got both of them back on their feet on Boxing Day, a miracle. Another gamble that paid off.

When the euro came into circulation in January 2002 the first official purchase using the coins and notes was on the French island of Reunion in the Indian ocean. It was for a kilo of Lychees. Changing suitcases of pesetas for notes as large as the five-hundred euro note, or the Bin Laden as it was known. You don't see them very often.

After lots of persuasion from my daughter it was time to start building the swimming pool. I ordered some books on the subject and we started planning the recreational facility. The size was going to be eight metres by four metres and a depth of one point five metres. Keeping the depth level is better for playing ball games as it means the person at the deep end doesn't drown while playing. There would be a slight slope to the bottom drain. If you are going to build a pool and have the chance of the bottom drain to use gravity to empty the pool, then use it. It's far easier than pushing the water through the pump, especially dirty water. Just turning a valve is cheaper as well. Get a good feel of the prevailing wind as you want to place the skimmers at the far end of the wind's direction and the jets at the other end so any surface debris gets propelled to the mouth of the skimmer box with the help of the breeze.

Trees and shrubs are not good near pools, not only are their roots attracted to the water source but also all the leaves end up in the pool.

I'm sure they get sucked in by some strange force. We built ours half in half out of the ground so we could have a sun deck around the pool water. Also, digging in our ground can reveal some very large boulders so a deep hole was not recommended. One of our mates was excavating a hole for his pool and revealed some bones that resembled that of human origin.

"Could they be Roman remains?"

"I don't think so," replied the digger driver.

"Why not?"

"During Roman times Bluchers and metal zips were not in fashion, they were popular in the late thirties."

"I suspect they are Civil War remains."

They got covered up quickly and a different site was picked for the pool.

The concrete shell for the pool is a complicated business, I would employ someone who has done it before. I have now built four pools, and each has been different. The pipework is basically a suck and blow network. The bottom drain, the vacuum line for cleaning and the skimmers are suck and the jets blow, also called the return. The pump should be situated below the height of the surface of the water. When installing the pipework always use high- pressure pipe, 50mm or 63mm in diameter. The glue again should be a specialised glue for this type of pipe. Take lots of photos of the pipe system and all the joints. The turnover rate of your pool is the amount of time it takes to circulate the whole volume of your pool. This depends on the diameter of the pipes used for your circulation system and the strength of the pump. During the busy time and hot temperatures, you need to circulate at least twice a day, this could be a couple hours twice a day.

Once the pool is rendered and if you have enough water, it is a good idea to fill it up. This can highlight any leaks and also the circulation system can be tested as well before covering up the pipework. When all is well and everybody is happy the coping stone can be put in place and the tiles you have selected stuck to the walls. Start at the top and work down, water always finds its own level. What happens below the surface is not that important, but to sit on a sun chair and stare at a water line that does not line up with the tiles is disappointing. We selected the small tiles that look lovely but take a lot of maintenance, a darker floor to attract the sun more and also a dolphin. The small tiles, 2.5 mil square need re-grouting often and cost a lot to apply compared to the bigger ones thirty-three centimetres square. Once tiled and grouted it is time to fill the pool up and enjoy. To fill our pool, we use the water from the acequia, it's spring water and very clean. Beware not all water from the acequia is clean. I was asked by a guest staying at our casitas to go and look at an old mill she was interested in buying. In the bathroom there was a sign saying, 'no paper down the loo please'.

I asked the owner, "Why is that, are the pipes too small to take it?"

"No," was the reply, "we don't like to see toilet paper in the acequia." This meant the human excrement was going directly into the irrigation system. Lovely.

With the sun shining and the water warming up the type of sanitation system to keep the pool water clean and safe has to be decided on, and at the time of building ours the copper ionisation method was popular. A chamber plumbed into the system with four copper and silver rods activated by a low voltage charge allowed the silver to be the bacteria stat and the copper to be algicide. All controlled by a very expensive magic box. This worked well until the pool water temperature was raised by the hot July sun and more and more kids turned up to use it.

The first problem was when Alex's lovely blonde hair turned blue. To get it back to blonde again she used tomato ketchup to neutralise the copper (don't ask me where that information came from). Trying to be chlorine free was a challenge and keeping the ph. to the ideal seven point two was difficult. To replace the copper rods which were meant to last a couple of seasons you needed a second mortgage. The system was soon taken out and just ordinary high-quality chlorine tablets were used.

Salt water systems were the next fad. The kit required is expensive and all you are doing is just turning salt into chlorine. Ozone came and went. I have found through experience that keeping the ph. at seven point two (the same ph. as the human tear), removing all organic matter on a daily basis, hoovering the bottom twice a week, no sun tan cream oil slicks and using a five in one tablet, the water can be kept fresh and enjoyable. The ph. is so important that keeping it at the correct level will make the chlorine ten times more effective.

Our daughter's birthday is early November, so a party was in order. She was coming up to nine years old and we always said she could have a big party every three years. So, invitations were handed out and a horde of kids were expected from many different nationalities. How to entertain this lot was going to be a challenge. After all the building work that was being undertaken, I noticed a lot of discarded workers' gloves. An idea came into my head, a glove hunt. We hid these discarded and broken gloves all over the place, but one marigold glove I filled with lots of loose change and threw it into the pool. The children were split into teams and off they went hunting the gloves. They all returned with their finds until one of them noticed the glove in the pool. November is not the time to go swimming, but as soon as Alex saw the glove in, she went like a pearl diver and retrieved the golden ticket. On another birthday we asked her what food she wanted.

"A buffalo," was the reply.

"A what?"

"You know, when people help themselves to plates of food." Ah, a buffet.

The method of hoovering the bottom can get complicated. you see very attractive looking robots that automatically wander around the floor and walls of the pool sucking up all the debris and dust that is naturally attracted to your recreational facility. They cost a fortune and rarely work as promised. You cannot beat the normal hose attached to a good quality cleaning foot and push it around until the floor is clean. The walls can be done with a brush. The amount of evaporation during the hot months will surprise you, this is one reason the town hall does not like swimming pools. When the water has evaporated you top it up with drinking water. This is fine when we have plenty, but in a drought year this valuable resource has be treated with respect.

The reward for all this hard work pays off when cooling off at the end of the day in the pool and watching the swallows swooping down to get a drink before heading home to their roost to be replaced by the hundreds of bats coming out from their hiding places: trees, caves, barns and abandoned properties, of which there are many in Órgiva.

If your neighbours are Spanish when you live in Spain then I expect you to get on with them well, they like foreign neighbours. They are not so keen on neighbours of their own race. An old Spanish story goes like this. A Spanish camposeno was walking along a track and noticed a lamp in the hedge. Pulling it out he gave it a rub and out popped a genie and gave the old boy quite a shock. "I'm the genie of the lamp and you can have one wish, but whatever you wish your neighbour will get double." After some thought the old man said, "Make me blind in my right eye!"

At last the guesthouses were running smoothly, and we found the time during the long summer holidays to place the caravan on a great caravan site on the coast at La Herradura (horse shoe) for the month of August. This very Spanish resort is only an hour away which meant we could easily come back for change over days at the casitas and little emergencies that needed sorting out. Spanish campsites are very friendly places with everybody chatting away and mucking in. We had a family group pitch up beside us, grandma, parents and kids. The parents would take the kids to the beach in the mornings while grandma prepared the lunch. Every day spot on two o'clock the family would return from the beach and grandma would serve out the lunch, and every day we got some as well.

You could rent a nice big fridge from the campsite and a TV if you wanted one. Every Spanish group on the site had a TV. One day we heard a bloke playing the pan-pipes pushing his moped along at the same time around the campsite. We watched with interest and discovered he was the mobile knife sharpener, putting his moped on its stand and engaging the grinding wheel to hone the knives. We also observed a bunch of Romany type characters re-upholstering seats and armchairs from their van. They just park up and people appear with all sorts of things that need sorting out. Avoids paying rates I suppose, and you can work in some beautiful places. On the beaches you get the normal peddlers trying to sell you anything from a rug to a carved elephant. It's not unusual to be disturbed at least six times while trying to enjoy your lunch at a beach chiringuito. A peculiar thing sold in the streets are socks. People walking around trying to sell a pack of socks. Strange.

Lazy hot August days were spent on the beach, taking the canoe out for a paddle in the bay getting to know some of the locals and of course Alex just mixing in with all the other kids chatting away in Spanish. One evening we heard the strumming of guitars and hand clapping that's associated with Flamenco music. Exploring the whereabouts of this spontaneous performance we came across a very large family of gypsies (gitano), some of them were very large, sat around in a circle playing away. They were evangelists from Granada. No alcohol was consumed, and no tents pitched, just loads of mattresses to retire to as the night closed in. The women had dark skin and arms the size of a retired Indian weight weightlifter, great saggy bingo wings flapping around as they clapped to the rhythm of the music. Only in Spain would you come across this sort of spontaneity. We continued going to La Herradura for a number of years and regard La Herradura as our second home in Spain, albeit in a caravan.

Getting back to serious work in September is always hard. It's interesting to see adverts on the telly and newsagents selling new magazines with hobbies such as collecting vintage cars or making a doll's house, it's sort of starting again, you have had your holiday now get back into your routine.

My BMW motorbike had been written off after it went over the edge of a cliff. Luckily the person who had been riding it had been able to abandon ship and was uninjured. A cheque arrived in the post from the insurance company and to Sarah's delight this money was to be used to build our bedrooms. The design was finalised and off we went again building our future.

Saint John the Baptist
June 24th
New Testament Prophet

PATRON OF ROADS, CANDLE MAKERS, FARRIERS, health spas, leather workers, road workers, wool workers, Jordan and Quebec.

Protector of lambs.

Symbol. The Eagle.

The prophet and evangelist, Saint John was born in the first century AD. He was regarded as a major religious figure. A prophet, an Evangelist. He was also known as John the forerunner and John the baptiser. He was known as the forerunner because he was the most religious man before Jesus. We normally celebrate saints on the day they die. But Saint John is celebrated on his birthday, coincidently this is six months before Christmas. He was regarded as our Lord's rival for the title of Messiah. John like many Hebrew prophets before him, had harsh words about the morals of royalty. Herod had him arrested, imprisoned and decapitated.

He baptised Jesus in the River Jordan. He met his end when the exotic dancer Salome performed in front of Herod at his birthday bash. Herod enjoyed the dance so much he offered the girl anything she wanted. Consulting with her mother, Herodias, she asked for Saint John's head on a platter. His relics are scattered far and wide, his head even made it to Halifax. The head ended up in northern France in 1204 in a city called Amiens. During a pilgrimage to York Minster the relics stayed the night in Halifax. A church was built on this site and dedicated to Saint John the Baptist. As patron to mid-summer, John has absorbed many of the pagan traditions. Bonfires to the gods on the eve of the day, Saint John's fire. The curative herb hypericum gathered at this time became Saint John's wort. And having sinners immersed in the waters of Jordan he became patron of health spas.

Our nearest celebration of Saint John the Baptist is in the spa town of Lanjaron. On the evening of June 23' the roads are shut, and people gather at the top of the main street and as the cannon goes off the drenching begins. Water is thrown from everywhere. Buckets are supplied, and tanks of water hold the ammunition. It's poured from balconies and from fire hoses. You get absolutely soaked. The horde parade through the town singing, "Agua, agua mucho agua." (Water, water lots and lots of water.) The streets resemble a river. If you go, take a change of clothes, it might be June, but you will freeze. You now need a ticket to enter into the celebration. The funfair is in town, the streets are lined with stalls of every sort and music blares out from all the bars. A really great experience. San Juan in Spain also marks the start of the summer holidays as the children break-up from school for ten weeks until September.

Another place to celebrate San Juan is on the beaches, all over the Spanish coastline bonfires will be lit and parties will go on all night long. We were in San Jose, Cabo de Gata one year on the eve of San Juan, enjoying a pizza, overlooking the beach and totally unaware of the occasion. We noticed people arriving with trailer loads of combustible material, and bonfires started to be lit. Soon we could count 25 and as darkness fell more and more became alight. We waited to see what was going to happen next, which was a lorry turned up, and swung open its back doors to reveal a massive sound system. The party was about to start. People appeared from everywhere, dancing, eating and drinking. As the church bell chimed midnight, they all walked into the sea. It took us a while to connect the bathing to the Baptist. Early the following morning bedraggled revellers slowly returned to the campsite resembling warriors returning from a battle.

Unsynchronised Traffic Lights

IN 2005 FERNANDO ALONSO BECAME THE first Spaniard to win the Formula One world championship. He drove a Renault. This was not a problem to most Spanish as the manufacturer was already popular in Spain. The Renault 4 was nick-named the four tins (cuatro latas) and just like in France they were useful in the campo. In France the low entrance to the back was good for getting your truffle hunting pig in and out. In Spain it was good for heaving your sacks of olives or almonds in for transportation. When Alonso moved to Ferrari, the sale of Ferrari merchandise boomed in Spain, but the cars were out of most people's budget.

Now Fernando drove very fast and very well, mainly because he knew it was one-way traffic. The young Fernando wannabes driving on Spanish public roads were not so lucky, but that does not stop them taking risks, overtaking on blind bends. If you leave a sensible gap between you and the car in front, it would be filled. You get overtaken on a treacherous piece of mountain road, putting you in danger and the driver of the super-tuned Seat, only for him to turn off a hundred metres farther on. Of course, on a Formula One car there are no indicators, is this why they are not used on the public roads? Only in towns when all four are flashed, as if to say 'my hazards are flashing, here I come and I'm immune from accidents because you can see me'. A little bit like in the old days when a man would warn other road users by waving a red flag in front of his boss's vehicle.

The first rain after the dry summer is always amusing, the roads become skating rinks and you notice the recovery vehicles are very busy. It's the same with spring rain and tarmac impregnated with olives that have fallen from overhanging branches making the road surface an emulsion of grease. With Spanish car insurance, recovery is included, as towing a vehicle with a rope is illegal.

We had a wet Easter one year and I asked a friend who owned a fleet of recovery trucks, "Had a good Easter then?"

"Golden rain," came the reply.

When a road sign says stop, STOP. You may be being watched. Easy money for Trafico (Guardia Civil Traffic Department). The same applies for tunnels, no matter how long or short they are, turn your lights on. They will be waiting! A continuous white line in the middle of the road may not be crossed.

Returning from England on my newly purchased motorbike I got caught behind a very slow-moving lorry coming out of Santander. I dropped it down a gear and sped past. Ten kilometres down the road I got pulled in and fined 60 euros. Two very polite officers on their motorbikes, and admiring we wore the same type of helmets, they enquired about my destination.

"Granada," I replied.

"Well you had better get a move on then," they said. The Trafico motor bike police always patrol in pairs, one of them specializes in mechanics and the other is a medic.

On the same journey, I arrived in Lanjaron right in the middle of Easter Thursday, smack into the parade. Having been in the saddle for an awful long time, I was keen to find my bed, and a very friendly police local directed me around the town thus escaping a long wait. Entering Órgiva I got stopped again.

"Where are you going?" was the first question. "Where have you come from?" the second.

"My bed," the first answer. "Santander," the second.

"Well you had better hurry then before you fall asleep."

All the Guardia I have come across have always been polite. But always remember they understand more English than you think!

A Spanish builder I have worked with bought himself a very nice Toyota Landcruiser. He had it a couple of years and then I noticed a green L plate in the back of the car, which meant a driving test had been passed and the green L had to stay in the back window for a year indicating the driver was a novice. So, I asked Bones (Huesos) who had passed their test. His reply stunned me. "All of us, myself, the wife, father and mother."

"But you have been driving for years," was my reply.

"Yes, we thought it was about time to take our tests, the police are getting hotter on checks!"

We were driving back from Malaga airport late one September night, around midnight on one of those high bridges they like building and suddenly I thought we were in a war zone. Now fireworks are nice to look at and enjoy when you are on the ground, but when you are travelling at 120km/h a couple of hundred metres in the air they tend to take on a different meaning. Bangs and flashes all around us made me think how the Spitfire pilots must have felt in the war. The village below, El Calla de Moral was having its fiesta. I hope they enjoyed it; it certainly woke me up.

On our way back from Madrid we needed to fill up and pulling into a service station, we lined up behind a car that was being refuelled. The driver goes off to pay. We wait and wait; he does not show so we then change lanes and refuel. When I went into the shop to pay, the driver of the other car was sat enjoying a cup of coffee. Just left his car at the pump. Amazing.

After your car is four years old in Spain you need to get an ITV (Inspeccion Tecnica de Vehiculos) (MOT). For the next six years this will be every two years, and then it will an annual test. When we first arrived the ITV stations, which are government run, would exempt foreign cars for the test, but that soon stopped as they realised that there was money to be made in making foreigners change the registration onto Spanish plates and encourage the purchase of Spanish-registered cars.

One day in Granada, we went to Trafico to attend the appointment we had been waiting 112 days for, to change our English driving licences to Spanish ones. At one desk and with our Spanish speaking daughter with us, my wife was told she needed her English national insurance number, which she did not have.

"Never mind," said the lady, "we can do it this way."

At my desk the lady said, "You cannot continue unless you have that number." She then stood up and left.

The other lady said," Come here and I will sort it out." After photocopies of all the docs and new appointments were made, we re-presented ourselves. "These medical reports are out of date. Never mind," said the lovely lady. "Passports please." We were not told to take our passports. (Our mistake, you should always have your passport with you.) "Never mind," said the ever increasingly lovely lady. After parting with 24 euros each we now had our temporary Spanish driving licences. Amazing. Conclusion; take everything you can when attending Trafico.

The MOT was introduced in the UK in 1960. The original idea was to have (like Spain) government run test centres. In 1950 an engineer, Robert Lovell was instructed by the UK government to devise a test for all vehicles to check on their road worthiness. He also advised the test centres be run by the Ministry of Transport. This was not taken and so there are 21,000 test centres in private garages around the UK, employing some 53,000 mechanics. The MOT is now paperless, but how many people got dodgy MOT's in the past and it is still possible now?

It's peculiar that a country like the UK thinks its above corruption and has open accountability, but a country like Spain knows it has a problem and takes steps to minimise it. The ITV can only be done on government-run sites. You pay your money and the vehicle gets checked and then you get a sticker if you pass. These stations are run by people who are not local to the area. If there is a school trip you pay the cost into a bank, not to the teacher, if there is a fiesta you buy tickets for refreshments and hand them over to the barman when you get your drink. Your tax (impuestos) is paid into the bank not directly to the Hacienda (tax office).

The Spanish tend to keep their cars much longer than the English, because to change ownership documentation in Spain is an expensive business. This also cuts down on the Arthur Daleys of this world flogging second-hand cars which can be expensive.

The driving school offices in your Spanish town can help in all matters of transport problems, they also have insurance franchises. A driving test and exam costs and comes in a package, 400 euros, in 2016. It's a theory first, thirty questions and you are allowed three wrong, followed by the practical. Two attempts in the package. The examiners went on strike due to the violence they faced when telling a pupil, they had failed, so they now get informed by e-mail. The only instruction on reversing is to enter a parking place. Hand brakes don't exist, and indicators are called intermittences and are barely used. After three years from passing you get your 125cc motorbike permit automatically. They run a points system but on count down not on accumulation. So, when you qualify you get eight points which will rise up to fifteen on good driving and no penalties. You cannot lose more than eight points in one day!

Scooters are a great way of getting around and in 2004 I noticed our bank had a deal on a Yamaha Neo forty-nine cc. Three years to pay, a free helmet and two years insurance included. Sounds good, so I spoke to our wonderful bank manager, Pablo. "Can I purchase a scooter for my wife for Christmas?"

"No problem," was the reply.

Papers were signed and I waited, this was in October. November came and went, still no scooter. In the middle of December, I had a chat with Pablo, who assured me it would be ready for the Three Kings.

"What!" I said. "We give gifts on Christmas Day the twenty-fifth."

"Well it's in Granada."

"Can I collect it?"

"Yes."

So off I went up to the builders' merchants with our Renault Kangoo to see if Manolo's Yamaha Neo would fit in. It did. Not only truffle hunting pigs fit in Renaults, you know! It turned out to be a very useful mode of transport. Alex, at the age of 14, passed her permit and used it to go to school. Selecting what car or mode of transport you will need is important, and this depends on what you end up buying. We ended up with a Renault Kangoo, a 4 x 4 and a quad, plus the scooter. Things seemed so simple when we moved.

The car tax in Spain is known as the permission to circulate, this annual expense goes direct to your town hall, not national. It was annoying seeing foreign cars for years being driven around our town with no tax, insurance or ITV. The local police now have apps on their phones to check for legality. Tax on fuel and the EU pays for new roads and the maintenance of the major highways.

In our town we have traffic lights controlling a narrow bridge and the main street. Three-way lights. This was taking life in your own hands, as when your light was green cars were still coming the other way. They could be dodged but if the public bus was coming through it was often a close shave. Armed with mobile telephones we went to each traffic light and phoned through the sequence. There was none, it was totally unsynchronised! We now have LED traffic lights and they are synchronised, and even have a camera to catch the red-light jumpers. The word for traffic lights in Spanish is semaforo (semaphore). Pedestrians be aware, zebra crossings are not recognised as safe places to cross the road. Do not expect the driver to stop as you step off the pavement. You have been warned. The gamble continues with flesh and blood.

Driving around the mountain roads and tracks is dangerous, with steep cliffs and precarious barrancos to fall into so you have to have your wits about you. The tight bends on some roads often mean you come face to face with another driver on the wrong side of the road. Fatal accidents are common and having a right-hand drive four by four has saved me on many occasions as I can get tight to the edge and see what I am doing instead of guessing. On narrow single carriageways, parts of the mountain roads have signs advising who has right of way. Common sense tells you traffic coming up a steep road gets right of way, especially if you are driving a lorry, but no.

I got a phone call one Sunday morning, it was Ollie, who lives up the mountain down a very tricky track. "Do you know anybody who has a tractor?"

"No, what have you done?"

"Parked the car last night in a rather silly place." I went up to inspect his parking skills, and it resembled the bus on the film the Italian job. "Don't tell the wife," Ollie exclaimed.

Thanks to three four by fours, a winch and a great deal of sweat, the vehicle was saved. Sometimes the camera on your mobile comes in handy and reminding Ollie of his parking skills with his wife nearby always seemed to earn me beer!

The Guardia Civil are creatures of habit just like most of us. They have their breakfast at 10am and their lunch at 2pm, so this is always a good time to travel if you don't want to be stopped, but they do like their road blocks and checks, so always carry your documents with you. There is a fine if you don't, sort of back to Franco times. Talking of Franco, when he was in power all towns, cities and villages had a street named after him, now they all have a street named Calle Libertade. I was stopped once without my licence on me, I received a ten euro fine. When I found my licence, I realised it had expired. That was lucky the fine would have been much greater otherwise.

The Guardia Civil's Saints day is on October 12th, Saint Pilar. Also, this is the day of Hispanidad. This is celebrated now as a national holiday and the boys and girls in green do it well.

Spain have several police forces. The Policia Local, employed by the town hall, they oversee official engagements minor crimes, planning permissions, parking tickets and local disputes. Dressed in black and armed. Known as Municipales.

The Guardia Civil reports to the Interior Ministry although this is a paramilitary force and has an association with the Defence Ministry. They mainly operate in the countryside and is a rural force. They have divisions to do with the traffic, mountains, border control, coastal patrol, environmental and fiscal. They wear green uniforms, are armed and are known as the green police. The Guardia Civil was formed in 1844 and mainly provided security to travellers against bandits. The section for the environment is called Seprona.

During the building of our house I was having a tidy up and lit a fire in an old oil drum to dispose of the many cement sacks we had accumulated. I was unaware that one of these sacks contained the plastic conduit pipes the electrician had discarded. Up it went, a plume of black smoke just as the Guardia Seprona went past. They took down my details and said I would be liable to a 6,000 euro fine. I went white with fright and tried to explain it was an accident. Two months later a friend in the town hall said I had a denuncia against me and unless I appealed the fine would need paying. A letter was written, and a photo of the oil drum was presented. That was the last we heard of the incident.

The badge of the Guardia Civil intrigued me, a sword and a bundle of sticks with an axe poking out of them. Researching this I found out that the sticks are called a Fasces Lictoriae and date back to beyond Roman times. The sticks are birch wood. It's a symbol of fascism and was used by Mussolini and many other organisations. It appears in the badge of the Swiss canton of St Gallen, in Lithuania, the British Fascist party and is used a lot in America. It's a symbol of a Magistrate's power and jurisdiction. The Cuerpo Nacional de Policia deal with major crime in large towns and cities.

Road rage is not common in Spain, yes you get the arm waving and normal fist pumping, but the incursion is soon forgotten, which is just as well as the hospitals would be full of victims. The saint hanging from the rear-view mirror will save them. They must look at their guardian more than they actually use their mirror. Hands-free mobile phones have meant they can wave both hands around when taking a call, even when they are driving.

Cars in the campo are a fairly recent occurrence. Sometimes you can get right up to the pedestrian before they get out of the way and then they split on either side of the road. It's quite common when they want to chat with a mate passing by to stop and natter not even aware you are waiting behind them. Pulling up at traffic lights is quite amusing, some stop as near to the middle of the road as possible, leaving a gap between them and the pavement wide enough to fit another car in. This is okay until an articulated lorry comes around the corner, then panic sets in as the lorry looms up and threatens to squash the front of their beloved motor. Parking outside a bar is fine, people don't think you are on the lash, you are just having a long coffee break.

I had a job to install some underground drainage pipes and a septic tank on a hippy commune. The Spanish digger driver was busy digging the trenches and me and my mate were laying the new pipes. This rather clean and attractive young lady appeared from one of the yurts, got into the digger driver's car and drove off. I wandered down to where he was working and asked him if his wife had arrived because some young lady had just driven off in his car. At first, he thought I was having a joke with him. Then he realised I was serious. We got into my car and sped off after the brigand. He was on the phone to the police, and as we went through town his car passed us on the other side of the road with this woman at the wheel. Turning around as soon as possible we found his car parked outside an hotel, locked but with a bag of dog food on the passenger seat. Strange. Eventually we located the young lady working in the kitchen of the hotel. By now Carlos had been joined by his angry father, and confronted the girl, who was Spanish. She explained she had done a car swap with another girl on the commune. The other girl just said the keys would be in the ignition of her car. She didn't even know what type of car she was meant to take but found the first one with keys in it.

Driving up a road wide enough for two vehicles but only just, when another car is coming down, you pull in and wait, then they pull in and wait. You could be there for ten minutes. I pulled in first doesn't seem to matter, they are dead scared of getting a scrape on the move. If you are stationary it's not your fault. Infuriating. If you get a wave of thanks for pulling in, it's normally a foreigner.

Alcohol is an everyday experience and drink driving is rife in the more rural areas. The alcohol limit is 50mg of alcohol to 100ml of blood. I have heard of many people getting breathalysed and being over the limit, but I have not known anybody lose their licence. A lady we knew in Nerja was pulled over late one night and breathalysed. Twice over the limit, the police asked her to follow them to the station. They kept her in until she was below the limit giving her coffee and toast and then told her to drive home carefully. There was another incident when a guy was caught and given a 600 euro fine. He did not have enough cash on him, so he was told to drive to the ATM and get it. Paco, a drunk from up the mountain, did lose his licence but was allowed to ride his scooter. When we first arrived, there was only one taxi in town and that was difficult to book, but now we have three which means no excuses anymore.

At the petrol stations it's quite normal to see coaches, tractors and lorries filling up with fuel. They don't seem to have private tanks on their premises. Órgiva Bus Company must have 20 coaches but no fuel tank of their own. On the farm back in England we always had our own supply, even though it was red! (Subsidised.)

Here is a letter that was published in a coastal English newspaper: 'Following on from all the comments in your paper recently about driving here in Spain, I have to say that, at last I've cracked it. Ladies are exempt from the ban on mobile phone use when driving! Avoid altercations with English-registered cars as two out of every three have no road tax, therefore no valid insurance. Ignore any perceived priorities on uncontrolled pedestrian crossings: he who dares, wins (driver or pedestrian). Parking on pedestrian crossings is OK. Parking vehicles in car parks is OK but only if you take up the space for two cars. Speed limits are merely advisory. Bull bars though banned in Europe can be fitted to vehicles (usually 4x4) here. Never expect to see a scooter with L plates. Accept that cyclists riding bicycles are free to ignore all traffic lights, can cycle on pavements and the wrong way on one-way streets. The use of indicators for all vehicles is optional, but when used can be left on indefinitely. Lane priority on roundabouts is well... mmm! With this knowledge assimilated I can now drive more safely in Spain and with a high degree of comfort making driving a pleasure rather than a chore!' Mike Thompson.

On the subject of indicators, a recent survey in the northern part of Spain revealed more than half of Spain's drivers do not use their indicators when they overtake or when they return. More than seventy percent do not use them when turning right and more than eighty-two percent do not use them when turning left. It is an offence and carries a 200 euro fine. I think if that was imposed as well as using the mobile phone when driving, the balance of payments would be in the green.

The standard of driving is what it is and like most countries they are different than what you are used to. The accident rate in Spain is less than the UK, because there are less vehicles and more space. You just have to adjust and be careful.

Summer Fiestas
Saint Carmen del Mar
July 16ᵗʰ

PATRON OF BOLIVIA, CARMELITES, CHILE, SEAMEN, fishermen and now scuba divers.

In the thirteenth century an English baron visiting Mount Carmel in what is now Israel, discovered a group of hermits/pilgrims looking for the cave that the Old Testament prophet Elias lived in. He brought them back to England and set up the order of the Carmelites. One of the members of the order, Simon Stock had a vision of Mary of Mount Carmelo, Stella Maris. The Virgin Carmen. The vision ordered that all men of the sea would be under her protection.

All along the Andalusian coast in fishing villages, Carmen del Mar is celebrated with elaborate floats paraded through the streets and loaded onto boats where she has a quick spin around the bay. In Malaga a statue of the Virgin is anchored to the sea bed and visited by scuba divers. It is believed that before her day the sea waters are not fit for bathing in and her presence will purify the waters, that's a tough ask in the Mediterranean. Whenever Alex, our daughter, invited her Spanish friends to the beach with us the parents would decline saying it was too early in the summer. Was it to do with Saint Carmen del Mar?

Saint Martha
July 29th

PATRON OF DIETITIANS, HAEMOPHILIACS, HOUSEWIVES, LANDLORDS, waitresses, butlers, cooks, servants and women workers.

Martha, Christ's hostess, was a bustling woman, always busy cleaning and cooking. Her symbol is a ladle. Her sister Mary on the other hand, was slightly more relaxed on the housekeeping side of things. Martha and Mary had a brother called Lazarus. Jesus arrived at their house and was told he was too late, Lazarus was dead. Jesus went to the grave and ordered the stone to be moved, but Martha said he would be a bit smelly by now. "Have faith," he said and sure enough the Resurrection of Lazarus was complete.

After the crucifixion of Christ, she left Palestine and went to Avignon, France. She began preaching and working miracles throughout Provence. She even vanquished a dragon. She tied it up with her girdle and ripped it apart. She died not long after she saw her sister ascend into heaven. Mary Magdalene. At least Martha did not have biscuits named after her!

In most Spanish towns you have barrios, areas of the town. Martha or Marta is celebrated by the barrio alto (high area) in Órgiva. A two-day fiesta centred around the market square and the old people's day centre. Nothing too elaborate, lots of music and dancing. But good to be seen supporting it.

Saint Cajetan
Santa Cayetano
August 7th

POVERTY-OBSESSED FOUNDER OF THE THEATINE order, 1547, patron of gamblers.

Cayetano, a lawyer and scholar was a priest in Rome and founded the Theatine order in an attempt to restore dignity to the clergy. (I wonder why.) His partner in this venture was Pietro Caraffa later Pope Paul IV of whom it has been said, 'If his mother had foreseen his future, she would have strangled him at birth'. Cayetano also had pawn shops in Verona, Venice and Naples. This may explain his connection with gamblers.

This fiesta was a surprise, the owner of the builders' merchants, Manolo, invited us up to his place just outside of town. He said they were having a small fiesta. His house backed onto a small private service road. Most of his family own a house on this road and a full-blown mini fiesta was taking place. Flags and bunting stretched across the road, a table football competition was in progress and there was great food and lots of beer. A small effigy of Saint Cayetano sat in pride of place. At five in the afternoon a section of the town band turned up and Saint Cayetano was paraded up and down the street, followed by some fireworks. An amazing afternoon.

Saint Filomena
August 11th

PATRON OF INFANTS, BABIES AND YOUTHS, destitute mothers, the living rosary and lost causes.

Born on 10th January 291 AD in Corfu, Greece and died on 11th August 304 AD in Rome. Filomena's tomb was discovered on May 24th, 1802 in the catacombs of Pricilla, Rome in an inscribed loculus (space hollowed out of rock). Inscribed on three tiles were 'peace be with you Philomena'. Her name means daughter of light. In 1805 Canon Francesco De Lucia Mugnano del Cardinate requested her relics for his oratory. In 1827 the Church got the three inscribed tiles as well.

Her father was a king of Greece and when Emperor Diocletian threatened war with Greece, they travelled to Rome to ask for peace. The emperor fell in love with Filomena, but she refused to be his wife as she had taken a vow of consecrated virginity. He tried to drown her by tying an anchor to her and throwing her into the river, but two angels cut the rope and carried her to the river bank. Then he ordered her to be shot with arrows, but the wounds healed, and the arrows returned killing six archers. In the end he had her decapitated. The chaplet of Filomena has three white beads for the Holy Trinity and thirteen red beads to represent her age.

Filomena is celebrated by the barrio bajo (lower area). The area below the schools near the bakers. It's a three-day bash, with the normal evening music and dancing, a mass in her honour and a procession. A programme of events is published. I was voted Mr

Filomena one year. I have the sash to prove it. Because it's held in August the events do not start until late and carry on long into the night. The baker does well as hunger sets in. On the Sunday lunch time a paella is cooked, large enough to feed everyone. One year the huge pan was set up on a tripod and the gas ring. As more and more ingredients were added the skinny legs of the tripod began to sag and the whole lot went crashing down onto the road. It was a miracle only a little was spilt and that nobody got burnt. The mess was cleaned up and the party continued. To gain Filomena's favours, a pink candle is kept alight.

Our friends bought a large old inn in this barrio and actually had the statue of Filomena in their galleried entrance hall. The church stole it in 2003 and claimed she flew into the church on her own. The Granada newspapers followed the story and even harassed three sisters who allegedly took the statue. The local people of the barrio raised some money and made a new niche in the street and commissioned a new statue from the saint makers in Motril. A celebration was held when the new figure arrived consisting of churros and chocolate.

The Virgin of the Snows
August 5ᵗʰ

SNOW FELL IN ROME ON THE night of August fifth as a sign to prove Mary Major was a saint. In the Alpujarras on the night of the fifth a pilgrimage takes place from the high mountain village of Capillaria to the peak of Mulhacen, Spain's highest mainland mountain standing at 3,478 metres above sea level. A collection of walkers, mountain bikers and mounted horsemen make the ascent and depending on the winter, quite often come across patches of snow still present.

The Feast of the Assumption into Heaven of Virgin Mary
August 15ᵗʰ

PATRON OF FISHMONGERS, HARNESS MAKERS, SOUTH Africa, Hungary, France, Paraguay, Jamaica.

This is the day the mother of Jesus ascended into heaven, body and soul. It is a national holiday in Spain. At the moment of the actual Assumption 'Doubting' Thomas could not believe it until Mary dropped an item of apparel into his hands. Such celebrations take place on this day as in France the seasons herbs are blessed, in Ireland you cannot drown on this day and in Almuñacar there is a huge firework display.

Nothing like a bit of sport

FROM AN EARLY AGE SATURDAYS MEANT watching or participating in sport. This included watching wrestling on TV with my dad. Jackie Pallo, Mick McManus, and Big Daddy were some of the stars to follow. Then off down to the town to buy fish and chips for tea. Later it was a treat to go to the Conservative club to enjoy half a pint of shandy and watch Match of the Day in colour. Football grabbed my attention while at primary school and West Ham were the team to follow. I suppose it was West Ham as they had a large proportion of players from the World Cup winning team in 1966. I went to our local sports shop and ordered a replica kit, the owner phoning up my mum to confirm it was OK!

At secondary school football got the boot and rugby took over, struggling to get into the under 12 fifteen but ending up as college captain by the age of 16. Then it was St. Austell technical college for a year and again captain of the side, playing at hooker. Launceston Colts were reformed, so some weeks it was three games a week, college old boys, St. Austell tech and the Colts. Surprised I had time to study!

My chosen vocation, farming, kept me fit for core strength, but I ran one hundred kilometres a week to have the stamina to enjoy and excel for the whole eighty minutes of a game. There were no substitutes in those days! We spawned an international from the Colt's team, Graham Dawe. One of the fittest, most aggressive, committed players I have come across. He only won five England caps but sat on the bench a record 42 times. Definitely an unsung hero.

During the summer months I got involved in athletics and the four hundred metres was my distance. I had a personal best of fifty-eight seconds, representing Cornwall and winning medals. I also represented Cornwall Rugby as a colt. When returning from agricultural college I made my senior debut for Launceston on the wing at Penryn. This all came crashing down when I was 23 and arthritis was diagnosed in my right hip.

I left Cornwall and moved to Somerset to manage a dairy herd of 220 beasts. The local rugby club, Castle Cary, got hold of me and I became their coach. Attaining coaching certificates from the RFU and being slightly more ambitious than the players I had to work with was frustrating, but the lads were great fun to be around.

So, moving to Spain was a shock, no sport. Not even Grandstand to watch on a Saturday afternoon. The wife would wonder why I was so grumpy on Saturdays. A longwave radio was purchased and at least I could listen to the football results. Órgiva was not a very sporty town. The foreigners that moved here were more yoga and meditation types. Conversations in the bar were never about sport but more about holistic massage and sweat lodges.

To watch the Six Nations rugby, we had to travel to Nerja to find a sports bar with satellite reception. It made a good excuse to get away from the mountains and appreciate the coast. On one such trip there was enough interested parties to justify a mini bus, the nearest bar now showing the match being The Hide-away in La Herradura. The match was England versus Ireland and it was being played on a Sunday, March 30th 2003. The grand slam decider.

We all gathered up in town leaving early enough to enjoy a good lunch before kick- off. We waited and waited, but no bus. As the organiser I was attracting some flak. The bus company was situated in Tablones, so off I went in my car to track down the driver. I found him still in bed, he had forgotten to move his clocks forward. He eventually turned up at great relief to me, so off we set. There was still time to grab a lunch and having the girls with us and to placate their disturbed Sunday it was their choice of restaurant. They picked the one farthest away from the bar.

With kick-off approaching and still plenty of meat left on our legs of lamb I decided it was time to make a run for it with the lamb in my hand. It's a long way from one end of La Herradura Bay to the other, so I stuck my thumb out and a car pulled straight over. Three of us clambered in clutching onto our unfinished lunch and got dropped off outside the bar.

"How long have you known him?" Steve inquired.

"Just," I replied. What lovely people.

Now with the internet and satellite I can watch it from my own lounge. There is even a Spanish bar in town that broadcasts the Six Nations. The commentary is in Spanish which means I'm relieved of listening to Eddie Butler, Brian Moore and the squeaky Jonathan Davis!

Things improved rapidly when the internet arrived and sitting in my tiny office following the latest action was a treat in itself. Órgiva was waking up to the fact that sporting activity could attract people to the area. Nearly all Spanish towns and villages have a small sports pitch, usually a hard court, so no fundraising was needed by the locals. National government decreed that all citizens should have access to sports facilities. A 16km run was organised by the town hall, from Órgiva to Lanjaron and back again. Now in its twelfth year it had nearly 1,000 participants this year.

Órgiva, in recent years has been well funded by national and local government for sports facilities. A very large hall originally constructed to house the weekly market (which the traders rejected) was the focal point for an area to be transformed into a sports centre. The building itself was turned into a multi-functional sports hall. Outside an artificial football pitch with flood lighting, a basketball court, a paddle court and a huge swimming pool was erected. The pool is a wonderful facility but only open in July and August. The locals say it's too cold to swim in June and in September the children go back to school. Such a shame as lots of the older generation would love to swim as part of their daily exercise.

The ski resort is only ninety minutes up the road, and from our house you can see the southern side of the Sierra Nevada covered in snow for most of the winter. Being keen skiers, it was our aim to give our daughter the chance to learn. One day in town I was talking to a Spanish woman telling her we were off skiing, and she asked me where! Alex soon picked up the skill and we made frequent visits to the slopes, often during the week, because we could.

One year we went up to town and noticed some activity with barriers and a lot of police around.

"What's going on?" I asked a local plod.

"It's only the Vuelta de España coming through town," he replied. The Spanish equivalent of the Tour de France. It's only!

In France it's a major honour to have the race come through your town. We settled down with a beer and waited, and the cavalcade that followed was incredible, I have never seen so many Guardia Civil cars and motorbikes before. The riders streamed past at such a pace you would think they have hidden engines somewhere. They were on their way to Granada and then up to the ski resort.

Rather them than me, I thought. It's happened again three times the latest occasion being this year.

Horses play a major role in Spanish society, with horseracing mainly taking place in the north. Mijas did have a track, but every year on the sandy beaches of Sanlúcar horseracing takes place on August 1st, 2nd and 3rd. We did have an annual racing event in a small village called Lobres. Two horses at a time up a track for about a kilometre. Great fun. One year the commentary was taken over by a young girl explaining that Mummy was too drunk to continue!

Bookies, there are no high street betting shops like in the UK, plenty of lottery shops though, and of course betting on line or apps on your phone. This takes away a hobby a lot of pensioners indulge in, in the UK.

Fishing in Spain is difficult, to obtain a fishing licence you need to pass an exam on the different species, life cycles and environmental issues to do with fish, in Spanish. Along with your licence you will need your permit to fish and insurance. The easiest way to dodge this is to go on an organised sea fishing trip. We were on a beach many summers ago and Alex wanted to learn how to fish. We had bought a cheap fishing rod with all the paraphernalia required (no licence needed to purchase) to give it a go. At the time we had a distinctive car that had yellow and white stripes on it (Renault test drive car). Well a friend of ours from the Guardia Civil in Órgiva was on secondment for the summer on the coast. Recognising our car, he decided to pay us a visit on the beach (it was a very small beach).

"Alex, this is how you cast the hook out to sea with the bait attached."

A firm finger tapped me on the shoulder and turning around all I saw was the green uniform of the Guardia Civil. Looking up to the officer's face, Antonio was all smiles and the wife was in hysterics sitting on the beach behind us. I had to enter the sea to sort my shorts out! He then proceeded to show Alex how casting was really done.

Hunting is very popular here in the Alpujarras. Every Sunday during the season, which starts on August 15 (pigeons and doves) you can witness a small army of shooters dressed in military fatigues having coffee in the Bar Mirasierra before they set off for their weekly walk. Four by fours parked outside with trailers laden with yelping dogs ready for their spell of freedom. The huntsmen belong to a club called the Cazadoras of Sierra Lugar. Their targets are mainly partridge and wild boar. This is classed as rough shooting. Not like the driven shoots you see in the UK. Once a year in November they have a special day when an organised competition is held. I was lucky enough to be invited to walk with a couple of Spanish friends and join in the lunch held afterwards. What an experience that was!

Miguel was aware I had been involved in country sports in England and I had a springer spaniel that enjoyed retrieving. So, one Saturday in the bar he ran I got the call.

"Andy, next Sunday would you like to come hunting with your dog?"

"That would be brilliant," I replied. "What time and where?"

"Five-thirty, Bar Mirasierra."

This is when the wife fell over with laughter. Well early mornings are not a problem for me as for fifteen years I arose at 4.30 to milk the cows. The following Sunday off I set with a full hip flask, packed breakfast, lunch and a sleepy confused dog. The bar was heaving with the great and good of Órgiva. Bank managers, businessmen, farmers, indigenous dark-skinned guys, policemen, and of course Miguel. I got lots of nods and buenos dias, a coffee and brandy were thrust into my hand and the chatter got intense. Lots were drawn and off we set into the darkness up the mountain in the Landover. The dogs in Miguel's trailer were a mixed bunch: a German shepherd, a pointer and a Bretton spaniel. My posh English springer spaniel was allowed to travel in the car. Up and up we travelled, Miguel's car altimeter read 926 metres above sea level. Off the road and on to a dirt track bouncing along as light began to appear in the eastern sky. Miguel's hunting partner was my old friend Antonio (Guardia Civil) from the beach experience. The car lurched to a halt and we had arrived at our allotted hunting area. The dogs were let out of the trailer and with great excitement and relief emptied their bowels ready for the exertions ahead of them. The temperature at that height and at that time on a November morning was to say a bit fresh.

Guns at the ready off we set. I stayed close to Miguel and my dog stayed even closer to me. Within forty minutes the first shots were fired, a volley of at least ten. Next thing I was aware of was a large pig running straight towards us, its tusks quite visible. My dog took one look and hid behind me. Miguel raised his gun and the boar stumbled and collapsed into a heap not twenty metres in front of us. Welcome to hunting Spanish style.

Okay, we have three dead boar, two juveniles and an adult. Weighing collectively just under 200kg. We are on a mountain side on a sunny but chilly November Sunday.

"What next?" I asked. Antonio explained this was his uncle's land and a track was just a hundred metres down there. "Excuse me but I forgot to bring my abseiling gear." Anyway, using dog leads we managed to drag the dead beasts down the precarious mountain side while Miguel set off to fetch his car and trailer. Exhausted I sat down and had some breakfast while Antonio proceeded to hang up the pigs and gut them. I don't exactly know the diet of a wild boar, but it stank. And I mean it stank, it would put you off eating wild boar for life. I had to bury my nose into my hip flask to distract my urge to vomit. Even the dogs took no interest in the offal. Miguel turned up with his car and the carcasses were hauled into the trailer. We set off again and a brace of partridge was bagged, but no more boar thankfully. Returning to Tablones, the enormity of the hunting party was plain to see. It resembled the scruffiest militia all dressed in camouflage. Four by fours parked everywhere with dogs in the trailers trying to grab a nap after their morning's exertions. The organisers were noting down all the morning's kills.

A dog competition was taking place for the best pointers. A small bird was released and then the dog and its owner had to scour the scrub and when the prey was found the dog pointed so the bird could be flushed out. Miguel entered me and my spaniel, Maisie. We set off with my dog obeying hand signals and the whistle. Maisie, on locating the bird and not being a pointer just rushed into the bush, flushed the bird, caught it and brought it to me unharmed. This got a round of applause but no prize as she did not point.

After all this excitement it was time for a beer and lunch. All the tables in the bar had sheets of plywood placed on them and were then covered with paper tablecloths. Tapas first, jamon, chorizo, artichoke hearts, olives and of course, bread. This was followed by goat stew (choto) and gallons of dark rose wine (costa). I was the only foreigner there, so my Spanish improved dramatically as the wine and food was devoured. Dessert was cold rice pudding (arroz con leche).

The tables soon got cleared away and next on the agenda was the prize giving. There were all sorts of categories with nearly everybody receiving something. Dog food, cartridges, T-shirts, more camouflage jackets and caps. I had donated a leather cartridge belt which was presented to an older gentleman and to this day he still says hello. The cards were out now, whiskey and Coke were the preferred libation and the bar was thick with cigar smoke. Antonio was busy butchering the wild boar outside on the pavement to the disgust of some passing vegetarian hippies. Wild boar carries a parasitic disease called Trichinosis. This is a roundworm of Trichinella type. All wild boar meat is tested for this parasite before human consumption. The infection is caused by undercooked meat containing the cysts of the Trichinella, so samples are sent off for analysis before the meat is consumed. The wife eventually rescued me and the dog as I gradually fell under the influence of a heady day's adventure. I still get invited, but only go to the lunch these days.

November the 1st is All Saints Day (El Dia Los Toda Santos) and a public holiday. We were showing some friends around and came across a Fiat Panda four by four with three dead wild boars strapped to the roof. The blood from their nostrils was trickling down the windscreen and a couple of dogs inside the car were going bonkers. Upon witnessing this strange sight, we went for a drink and inside the bar was a very proud huntsman with a large freshly shot Ibex head. The local police were there as well as the Guardia Civil and the mayor. This guy had a licence to cull this animal and photos were taken and everything recorded. Getting a gun licence in Spain includes education of what you are hunting and the environmental impact of the animals you are after.

Football is obviously very popular and a very nice all-weather pitch with floodlights has been installed and is in constant use. It's been great to join in the success of the Spanish national football team.

England won the World Cup in 1966, but I was too young to appreciate the event so, Spain winning the Euro twice in 2008 and 2012 and becoming world champions in 2010 has somewhat compensated for the inadequate performances of the so-called inventors of the game.

We were following a Spanish game during the 2008 Euro campaign in a little bar and on winning, the barman decided to celebrate with some small explosive devices. He had three bangers lined up on the bar. One had been exploded already. I picked one up to examine, he had lit the thing so I threw it on the floor, but unfortunately for me it landed under the wife's chair. It went off with an almighty crash sending the wife into orbit. She was not amused, and I ended up with a very sore left ear! When Barcelona or Real Madrid win a cup or title, we normally know about it by rockets (cohetes) that are let off in celebration.

Rugby union is catching on in Spain, and it is mostly played in university cities, but with hot spots like Puerta Santa Maria, Barcelona and the Basque country. A team in Barcelona joined a league in London as it was cheaper to travel to England than the rest of Spain. We helped Marbella rugby club celebrate their 20th anniversary by attending a sevens competition. We took a bus load down and had a great day watching teams from Casablanca, Lisbon, Gibraltar, Spain and a couple of English sides compete.

The Spanish that went with us were more amused by the drinking games that took place after the sport! We went to Edinburgh to watch Scotland versus England in the Six Nations. Two Spanish, an Italian and us English. On the plane there was a touring party from Cordoba. At the moment, 26,000 people play rugby in Spain. Watch this space. I was in the local butcher's shop and a Spanish lady came in I knew. She knew I was into rugby and told me her daughter was playing rugby today in Belfast, as she was away studying in Limerick. Well I never thought I would have had that conversation when we first arrived in Órgiva!

From near sport wilderness Órgiva can now offer sports activity from karate, volleyball, rock climbing, canoeing, walking, paddle, gymnastics, swimming, mountain biking, road bike racing, body building, basketball, zumba, dancing, running, skiing, chess competition jumping off rocks into pools of water, this is called cannoning, (two people died this year) and yes, yoga.

You might come across brightly lit clubs but this has nothing to do with a bit of sport!

Saint Michael
September 29ᵗʰ
Archangel (Michaelmas)

PATRON OF AMBULANCE DRIVERS, BANKERS, COOPERS, grocers, hatters, paramedics, paratroopers, radiologists, police officers and Germany.

Saint Michael is a pre-congregational saint, like Saint Sebastian, meaning the Canonization of saints prior to the institution of modern investigations performed by the Congregation for Causes of Saints.

In the New Testament Michael leads God's armies against Satan's forces before the world was created. God's commander-in-chief, where in Heaven he defeats Satan.

Pope Leo XII had an out of body experience in which he saw Michael victorious over the horrors of hell. He wrote the prayer to the Angel Saint that is still recited at the end of every Sunday Mass.

Michael appears in the Koran and is described by Mohammed as having 'wings the colour of green emeralds covered with saffron hairs each of them containing a million faces.

Once, the Devil seeking revenge on his old enemy, flew up to earth, terrifying the workers of the Church of Saint Michael in Cornhill, England leaving his claw marks on the bells and the masonry.

Michael was even seen on the battlefields in France, Italy and Germany during the two world wars.

In Roman Catholic teachings Michael has four main roles: the leader of God's armies, the Angel of death, he weighs people's souls on perfectly balanced scales and he is the guardian of the Church.

Órgiva does not actually celebrate Saint Michael, but they do have their annual fair during this time. Originally based on livestock selling (Ganados) and horse trading. It was the time of year when farmers from all over the Alpujarras would bring their beasts down from the hills and mountains to be sold or traded.

During the fiesta, very proud horsemen and women dress in traditional country apparel and parade their prized steeds up and down the streets preparing for the ribbon race (Cintas) on the Saturday. Kids will do this race as well on pedal bikes, the aim is for the jockey or cyclist to spear the ribbon while travelling at speed on a tarmac road. The ribbon has a value written on it as the prize. Now, I have done quite a lot of horse riding and you get to know metal horse shoes and tarmac create very slippery conditions, so if you go to spectate keep your distance, six hundred kilos of horse and rider with no brakes sliding towards you is not funny.

It's a four-day party. Thursday through to Sunday. The bars spill out onto the streets, cooking all sorts of delights, and the aroma of freshly cooked sardines fills your senses. The ladies of the town dress in fantastic flamenco creations showing off the summer tan that they have been working on. The funfair is in town, street traders selling all-sorts of rubbish from realistic looking guns to mini explosive devices, and pop-up bars appear in car parks and vacant shops. Vending machines selling beer, and pinchitos stalls cooking marinated cubes of pork over charcoal burners, all appear out of nowhere. Free sombreros are handed out advertising a particular builder or a bar. A temporary bull ring is erected, although bull fighting has now stopped taking place in Órgiva. However, a kind of 'it's a knockout' competition takes place with teams of youngsters navigating an obstacle course with the close attention of some young frisky yearlings (young bulls) with horns. Horse shows with dancing Lipizzaners, art exhibitions, crazy car races, some very good rock bands, giant paella, traditional fried eggs with garlic with a competition on who can eat the most eggs, (twenty-four is the record), followed by a good dose of laxative, all can be enjoyed during the fair. The people of Órgiva have a nickname, los hueveros (egg people). Apparently on a visit to the town by the King of Spain, eggs were thrown at the royal visitor. Another story is the King arrived so late the streets were illuminated by egg shells full of olive oil acting like little lanterns. Most Spanish towns have nicknames (el apodo) for their inhabitants. In Lanjaron they are the cannonerous (cannons) in Tablones, tableros (planks). A pensioners' lunch provided by the mayor gets proceedings off to a flying start on the Thursday held in a huge marquee. The old people have their own day centre as well, and yes, they have their own bar and provide a very good menu of the day. Even foreign pensioners get invited to the town hall leader's lunch.

The traditional time for bull fighting is during the annual fiesta. In Órgiva this does not take place anymore but many years ago I was invited by my Spanish friend to attend the spectacle. A temporary bull ring was erected on a level field just outside town. I was instructed to meet at a certain bar at four in the afternoon and festivities started with several beers. Then it was time to wander down to the bull ring. Juan placed a sombrero on my head and shoved a great big fat cigar into my mouth. Not being a smoker, I found it difficult not turning green and throwing up my recently quenched thirst. One of our party had a whole leg of jamon over his shoulder, another guy had a bag full of bread and they all carried the leather wine bag. As we sat waiting for the fight, the jamon was expertly carved and passed along with hunks of fresh bread. The bota (wine bag) was passed along as well. The Spanish lads were waiting to see me spill it all over my shirt, but no such luck there, I had plenty of practice when working with them. Selecting the best seats so the sun was not in your face is important. In the large bull rings around the country, seats with shade sell for a premium, but our temporary metal bull ring had no such luxuries. The show began with the local fire tender arriving to a great cheer as water was sprayed on the dirt to keep the dust. The guy with the hose got a great reception but no white handkerchief. The first bull was ready to enter the ring, the town band struck up, the mayor was seated and ready and so was the captain of the Guardia Civil. The whole stadium shook with power as the bull raced into the ring charging at the matador who was wearing his suit of light (Traje de Luz). I won't bore you with the rest of the grizzly detail, but once the bull had been dispatched there was no ceremonial team of mules to drag the carcass out but only the local digger driver with his bobcat to scoop up the brave bull from the dirt where he had fallen. If the matador has done a good job the ears of the bull are cut off and thrown into the crowd. Alex, my daughter, caught one.

This nepotistic side show is slowly coming to an end in most of Spain but will never be forgotten. A quote from Jose Ortega: *'The history of bullfighting is intimately linked with that of Spain, such that, without understanding the first it is impossible to understand the other'*.

The bull that is bred for the so-called sport is not much use for anything else so will end up in some rare breeds farm being admired for what he was. Maybe the British fox hound will be with him.

An international migas competition is held on the Sunday in the woods next to the Rio Chico, much bigger than the Tablones affair. You enter your team by going to the competition table. You receive a number, a cup of migas powder, a cup of olive oil and a melon. Help yourself to some concrete blocks to make your fire pit with and grab some logs, light a fire and off you go. There are in excess of two hundred teams some years. Just a wander around the wooded park will fill your nostrils with wood smoke and the cooking of all types of local food you will never see in restaurants. You see groups of people with fridges, televisions, and whole jamons. Doing it better than your neighbour is the order of the day. Teams get T-shirts printed (there is a competition for that as well). Invariably you will get invited to join in with a group and sample their hospitality. It became international when we entered a team. Our first attempt resembled a yellow brick rather than a fine crumble. There always seems to be an old lady close at hand to show the stupid foreigner how to make it. The judging gets done behind closed doors.

There is a caretta competition. Let me explain. A caretta is Spanish for a cart. So, many of the local youths decorate a trailer or an old caravan with traditional flamenco patterns, old country artefacts, beer pumps, jamon stands and very loud traditional Spanish music powered by noisy generators. They are pulled by four by fours or tractors. Most participants are dressed in country garb or T-shirts specially printed for the weekend. The Charanga brass and drum band add to the atmosphere. The carettas are judged, and the winners receive more jamon and beer. The local wine is carried around in the bota bags, leather pouches with a nozzle on the end and offered generously. Getting the right amount of pressure on the bag is the secret in drinking the contents and not ending up with it all down the front of your shirt. Be careful the wine is normally costa. The carettas roam around the town adding to the carnival atmosphere. People are often dancing in the streets with the girls dressed in their fabulous flamenco gowns. There is bingo, and even a foot race in stiletto shoes. This is just during the day; at night the pop-up bars provide all types of music. Four stages provide a variation of acts with the main marquee hosting the latest local talent, some groups with national recognition. It's a special fiesta sort of marking the passing of summer and the start of the autumn.

Declarations, Birthdays, Unions
and Endings

"THIRTY EUROS A HEAD," SARAH EXCLAIMED, "that's ninety euros to attend a Spanish child's first communion." We had been invited to a Spanish friend's son's Holy Communion. Not knowing the protocol, we inquired on the correct way to approach such an occasion.

"Well it had better be good," I replied.

During May of each year the weekends are taken up with First Communions. This we found out when one Sunday in May we decided to go out for lunch. Everywhere was full of communion parties. We eventually found a restaurant with a spare table tucked away in a corner. The waiter said we would have to be patient. This gave us time to observe the party unfolding before us. The little girl's communion was attended by a couple of hundred folk all having a great time. The girl was dressed up like a junior bride, parading around with her mates and milking the event to the full. After the meal she did a tour around the tables with gifts for the guests, little photos of herself in a frame and in return brown envelopes were passed over containing the loot. This would go into her savings account if she was lucky, otherwise depending on the parents' wealth it would go towards the cost of the party. A two-piece band turned up and proceeded to entertain the congregation who were soon on their feet dancing away. We had this to look forward to when the invitation came our way.

The invitation was for a Sunday in the middle of May, the

communion in question was for our friend's son, Juan. "What time do you want us in church?" I asked.

"You don't have to come to church if you don't want to," was the reply.

It's true, if you go to any event involving a church not many will attend the service, but they will all attend the celebration that follows!

We went to church and witnessed Juan and a handful of other youngsters being put through the ritual of First Communion. Juan was dressed very smartly in a naval uniform, which most boys wear. The girls are always dressed as young brides. After the service we headed down to a function room called El Salon. To our surprise there were two other communion parties taking place in the same venue, just a simple partition separating the families. At this time our Spanish was very rudimentary, but our hosts placed us on a table with familiar faces and as the beer and wine flowed the communications became easier. At times like this you feel very humble to be invited at all, but having our daughter going to the local school helps so much with the integration and also, we imbibe in Juan's parents' bar. The meal was excellent and after the presents and photos the partitions were removed, and we all had one great big party together. Many more communion parties were attended and soon we were old hands at enjoying the feast of the communion.

Early 2004 a friend, who was a regular visitor to us in Órgiva was having his fiftieth birthday party back in England at the rugby club. Neil and Jackie had been good friends of ours for many years when we lived in Somerset, yet no invitation to attend had landed on our doorstep (so to speak). Chewing this over with Neil's favourite Spanish barman, Miguel, we hatched a plan to gate-crash the event. It was early January and we had ten days to plan the assault. Passports were not a problem for Miguel and his wife Nuria as they could travel on their identity cards (Schengen agreement). Accommodation in Somerset was organised with more frequent visitors to Órgiva that Miguel and Nuria knew. EasyJet tickets were cheap at that time of year and so was car hire. We were to fly out on the Saturday morning and return on Monday evening.

Early Saturday morning we set off for Malaga airport. Miguel and Nuria had never been to England before and spoke little English and ourselves just some basic Spanish but with all good friendships, lack of instant communication did not get in the way of having a laugh and a good time. We taxied and took off in bright blue sunshine, and once in the air Miguel extracted some tins of beer from his carrier bag (San Miguel of course) and I tried to explain you can't do that, you have to buy the airline's beer. He shrugged and carried on drinking. When landing in Bristol we were welcomed by the same colour skies we had left behind in Malaga although a tad colder. Amazing! We had warned our Spanish friends that wind and rain were the norm. At the car hire office, we collected the upgrade. Instead of a small economy we got a large luxury.

Off to the Mendip Hills to a pub called the Huntsman's to meet the people we were staying with and to have an English pub lunch. Our English friends had three children, so we had to dine in the family room out the back. The cold crisp January day got even better for Miguel as the local shoot had just finished their day's hunting and a brace of pheasant was brought in for the pub by the gamekeeper dressed in his tweed plus fours and jacket. Not the military fatigues that you see in Spain.

After a hearty lunch of faggots, chips and mushy peas, all home-made, I gave Miguel a tour of the establishment once owned by the actress Diana Dors. The inglenook fireplace in the public bar was ablaze with a roaring log fire surrounded by a few locals with their collie dogs and a spaniel at their feet and pints of cider in old stone mugs. Miguel was a little confused, dogs are allowed in the bar, but children have to be in a separate room. "You have strange priorities," he said.

Next stop was the cathedral city of Wells, Sarah's home town. With the sun still shining but getting lower the façade of the cathedral looked stunning and literally took our friends' breath away. On entering the building, the choristers were in full voice in the nave. It was like it had been pre-arranged. Sarah had never heard the choir sing like that in all the time she had lived there. After this place of worship, we took them to another, the City Arms pub to sample a drop of local cider.

Then it was off to our accommodation, a village house that used to be a mill. Miguel could not believe it, staying in a Molino, with a pub next door! The taxi arrived and we set off for the party. Our friends Peter and Helene entered first, they were gate-crashing as well, next went Miguel and Nuria and finally ourselves. It was priceless the expression on Neil's face. Our Spanish guests soon mingled and found out the wife of the rugby club's coach was Spanish. They had a good laugh looking at the team photos on the wall, especially of me with a hair-do resembling that of Michael Jackson.

"Who is the old lady over there?" Miguel inquired.

"That's Jackie's mum, she is eighty-two years old," I replied.

"How long has she been smoking dope?" he asked.

What! After much dancing and drinking it was time to head home.

The following morning and a proper English breakfast inside us, Miguel declared he had fourteen pints of Stella last night. Nuria confirmed the fact with a wiggle of a limp little finger. After a stroll around the village, it was off to the pub for the inquest of the party held the night before. Miguel decided to sample the roast beef lunch and we all had a laugh about Jackie's mum trying out marijuana for the first time. The day was Robert Burns day, January twenty-fifth and our hosts laid on a fantastic supper of haggis, turnips and mashed potato. Quotations of poetry and some very nice Scottish wine followed. All very confusing for our foreign guests.

On the Monday we packed our things thanked our hosts and set off for Yeovil. A bustling market town, where one of those street sellers stopped me, asking if I would like to donate by banker's draft to Oxfam. I replied in my best Spanish, and she soon scuttled off, leaving

Miguel in a bout of laughter. A fish and chips lunch followed in the famous Palmers fish restaurant, then having nearly exhausted the complete range of British cuisine we headed off to the airport.

On our late return to Órgiva, the bar was still open that Miguel is a partner in, so a full recount of the weekend took place. The conclusion was, they treat their dogs better than their children, the bread is strange, the coffee weak but the Stella is good, and the weather is not as bad as they make out. I often hear Miguel talking to his friends about his weekend in England.

He would ask his mates, "Have you been to England?"

"No," would be the reply.

"It's a strange place, no wonder they all want to come here."

My fiftieth birthday was fast approaching, and as it was in the middle of May we decided to have a party at our house. After some discussion on the way to feed a lot of people we settled for a lamb spit roast. A warning to the innocent when researching spit roasting on Google. Be aware! As this was out of burning season, I asked the local police if it was OK to cook a lamb over an open fire in May, and they said fine as long as they got an invite. Once finding the proper page on spit roasting, I began to realise my error. To cook an 18kg lamb, stuffed with garlic, rosemary, pistachios, apricots and rice ready for lunch means lighting the olive wood fire at 5am. Attending and turning the thing constantly until ready for serving slightly spoilt my birthday morning, but with help from some mates keen to learn about spit roasting the result was fantastic and a great party was had by all.

Christmas celebrations are a refreshing change. Although the Christmas lottery tickets go on sale at the end of June the event is hardly mentioned until the early December holidays of the day of the Constitution and the Immaculate Conception, December the sixth and December the eighth.

To say 'happy Christmas' in Spanish is 'Feliz Navidad' and the reply will be 'igual amentae" equal to you. The festive lights are hung in the high street around the middle of the month of December and belens appear in shop windows and the front rooms of houses with big windows. A belen is a nativity scene depicting the stable and the three wise men visiting the new-born prince. Family heirlooms are dusted off and displayed with one-upmanship being the order of the day. If you study the display carefully enough you should see a figure having a poo. This could be a member of the Royal family, David Beckham or even Donald Trump. They say it makes the children look at the scene. The town hall run a competition and award prizes to the best display. No doubt a jamon. Houses do not get plastered with lights like you witness in other parts of Europe although you will see the odd Santa Claus clambering up a balcony railing. No Christmas trees either, although all of this commercialization is creeping in. Mid-night mass is held in the church on Christmas eve, this is known as La Misa de la Gallo. The mass of the cockerel. Allegedly a cockerel crowed all night during the birth of Jesus.

Bars will put their decorations up a couple of weeks before the big evening and have large wicker baskets full of all the goodies associated with feasting: cava, salami sausage, whole legs of jamon, turron, whiskey, caviar, sugar almonds, as raffle prizes. There is a pre-printed page divided into one hundred boxes from zero-zero to ninety-nine where you buy your number and write your name in. The cost per ticket can vary depending on the quality of the produce, the winning number will be the last two digits of the first prize of El Gordo which is drawn on December the twenty-second. A bar called Four Corners (Cuatro Esquinas) always has a wonderful Christmas decoration display, but the Christmas after the landlord died the place was bare as a sign of respect. We all miss you Elias.

Traditional Spanish Christmas songs are piped over the loud speaker system throughout the town during the festive season and you sort of expect Ruth Madoc to interrupt the melodies with, "Hello Campers," from the sitcom, Hi De Hi. We have a lot of choirs in town and they all come together to put on a great evening in the church a week before Navidad, singing and performing various Christmas songs from Noche de la Paz (silent night), Ande la Marimorena and the kids' favourite, Los Peces en el Rio (the fish in the river) with vigorous tambourine bashing to accompany the tunes. The town band always put on a great show as well.

Christmas Eve (Noche Bueno) is the most important time for all Spanish families at Christmas as sons and daughters return home from working abroad or in nearby cities and gather to consume mountains of prawns the size of lobsters and roast suckling pig all baked in a blanket of salt using the outside olive wood fired oven. We have been fortunate to have been invited to this Good Night ever since we arrived in Spain with our Spanish friends. Presents are exchanged. Angeles's mother is always there helping with the food and clearing up. We have always known her as Maria, so it came as a bit of a shock when her name was called out for a present only to be called Angelita. We apologised for calling her by the wrong name for so long.

She shrugged her shoulders and said, "I have been called a lot worse in my time."

After such a huge feast the whiskey comes out and the dancing starts. Juan's nieces put on a great choreographed routine that Juan seems to know as well!

Christmas Day is a holiday, but all the bars are open for business. We Brits get a second feast as we generally do the Christmas Day thing along with friends and some Spanish mates who want to experience Christmas Day English style. There is no Boxing Day in Spain, and life's routine returns without much fuss.

December the twenty-eighth is the Spanish equivalent of April Fool's Day. El Día de los Santos Inocentes. This day is observed throughout Spain and the rest of the Spanish speaking world in much the same way as April Fool's Day. When a joke is played on you the joker says, "Inocenti, inocenti!" Television stations and newspapers will broadcast or print 'news stories' based on humour rather than fact.

In its origins the Day of the Innocents comes from the gospel of Matthew in the Bible. King Herod ordered the slaughter of all baby boys under the age of two in Bethlehem because he was afraid the baby Jesus would become his rival. Joseph and Mary had already taken the baby Jesus away to Egypt, so the 'joke' was on Herod, and thus followed the tradition of tricking friends on that day. The sad story of the babies being murdered makes them to be the first Christian martyrs. If you are patted on the back by a Spanish friend on this day, I expect you will have a white cut out figure stuck to you!

In a town called Ibi, near Alicante they have a tradition that goes back more than two hundred years to celebrate this day. A massive food fight. The festivities traditionally begin around eight am when the participants dressed in mock military uniforms stage a mock coup and take over the town. The townspeople then regain control with the food fight taking place. The fiesta is known as Los Enharinados, 'the flour covered ones.

New Year's Eve or Nochevieja (old night) is celebrated slightly different in Spain compared to the UK. There is no build up during the evening, they mostly stay indoors with family, have a meal and watch the bells on TV. To say Happy New Year in Spanish is 'Feliz Ano Nuevo'. When they do get out it's lucky to wear red underwear and also to eat twelve grapes as the clock chimes in the New Year. Small seedless grapes are advised so you don't choke to death before the New Year starts. Cava is drunk and the party starts. Us Brits that started too early retire just as the Spanish get going. New Year's resolutions don't happen as the Three Kings celebration is yet to come. It's lucky to eat lentils on New Year's Day.

The feast of Epiphany is traditionally Spain's main festive holiday. It is believed that the Three Kings travelled from the area of Cadiz when they visited the stable led by the star all the way to Bethlehem. This is when children receive their presents not from Santa but from the Three Kings. The night of the fifth of January is when the great parades take place all over the country, and floats carrying the Three Wise Men (Los Reyes Magos) travel through the streets throwing sweets (painful when you get one in the eye) and other small gifts to the waiting crowd. Children hold up upside down umbrellas to catch as many as possible. In our small town the Three Kings end up at the old town hall sitting on their thrones to hand out presents to the eagerly awaiting children. The parents would have bought the gifts and added the kids' names to the list. You can imagine the mess created by the frantic unwrapping of the gifts. Sixty-seven percent of Spanish children prefer to receive gifts from the Kings rather than Santa. On the day of the sixth they tuck into a special cake called a Roscon de Reyes. A cake baked in a ring shape and decorated with candied fruit and hiding something inside. A small toy and a broad bean. Whoever gets the toy is crowned king or queen and who gets the bean has to pay for next year's cake. A famous Spanish store one year hid two hundred and fifty small gold ingots in their cakes. A nice surprise for some people. The other Christmas draw takes place on this day as well, El Nino with six hundred and thirty million euros up for grabs. The draw takes place in Cadiz! After all this celebrating the children return to school.

The first Spanish wedding we attended was in Motril, in 2006, and the guy who made our granite work surface for the kitchen invited us. Jose.

We have an in-house joke about the Spanish, it's like they ask each other, "Have you got one yet?"

"One what?"

"A pet foreigner."

I think we were his. We hadn't even met his intended. The wedding was to take place in the middle of August. Coaches were laid on to take us to Motril mid-afternoon. Dressed in our finery and melting in the summer heat we all gathered at the bus stop in Órgiva. I had a tie on but noticed many guys didn't bother. Three bus loads made the way to the church in Motril centre. Waiting for the bride and groom to appear I noticed most of the men were wandering off. I went into the church for the service, but apart from the groom and the immediate family I was the only bloke there. The rest had buggered off to the fiesta. When the ceremony was finished, and everyone had moved outside the menfolk started to reappear. As the newlyweds emerged from the church, they protected themselves with their decorative parasols from the bombardment of rice and uncooked chickpeas thrown at them by the reunited congregation. Up on the parapet of the building, lines of pigeons awaited a fine supper.

We all got back on board the coaches, my thirst somewhat more urgent than the other hombres and off we set for the reception. This was to be held in a converted sugar refinery. An amazing venue. Sugar cane has been grown in the area for a thousand years, brought here by the Moors and is the only place in Spain where it has been successfully cultivated. But alas no more, sugar beet is far easier to grow and process. The Larios family (of gin fame) bought the refineries and continue to this day producing Palido Rum.

At the reception more and more people turned up, the church bit obviously not important. Canapes were offered and the thirst quenched. After a fantastic meal the brown envelopes were exchanged for big fat cigars and parcels of sweet candy-coated almonds. "Viv as los Nobis," (long live the sweethearts) chanted the four hundred guests. "Que se besen," (kiss the bride). Before we knew it, the coaches turned up to transport us back to Órgiva. Five o'clock in the morning.

The next wedding invite was a little farther away, Romania. My labourer, Stefano was getting hitched in his home town of Lasi, pronounced Yasi, in the province of Moldavia, Romania's second largest city. There are a lot of Romanians living and working in Órgiva, filling the labour vacuum by charging less than the Spanish and working in the black. It always amazed us how they picked up the Spanish language so quickly. While we were travelling in Romania, twice in our hotels, we had no hot water. So, Spanish for not having hot water is, 'No tengo aqua caliente'. In Romanian, 'Nu tiene apa calda'. Very similar don't you think?

"How are we going to get there?" Sarah inquired. Sarah had

contacted her birth mother (having been adopted) and this woman was going to be in England in early August. We could travel to England, meet Eileen, fly to Budapest, hire a car and drive to Romania. So that's what we did. Via France for a camping holiday. The meeting with Sarah's birth mum went well and we were soon on our way to Hungary.

"Alex, you will have to do a project about this trip." No response.

Getting into Romania was as difficult as it was for the Romanians to get out, a two-hour wait at the border. We had to show the guards the wedding invitation. To get Stefano and Maria back to Spain we had to get a Spanish notaria to draft a special invitation to prove they had work when returning to Spain. After nine days touring beautiful Romania we arrived for the wedding. Moldavia is about as far away from the Hungarian border as you can get. We visited the famous Painted Monasteries in the northeast of the country, near the town of Suceava, Sighisoara the home town of Vlad the Impaler (Dracula) in Transylvania and many delightful villages lost in a time warp. Horse and carts were the main mode of transport and if the signpost said forty kilometres to our destination then due to the state of the roads it would take the best part of an hour (no different from England I suppose). We even came across two hairy guys on motorbikes saying they were chefs filming a series for the BBC. The large towns were horrible and neglected. The blocks of flats were falling to pieces, great water pipes ran alongside the streets supplying hot and cold water to these apartment blocks and during Nicolae Ceausescu's dictatorship the water could be turned off at any sign of trouble, and during the very cold winters to have your heating was very important. Control.

The wedding itself was an experience we will never forget. The day before the event we drove out to Maria's father's farm in a small village called Gura Bohotin overlooking the plains towards Russia. After the guided tour of the farm, a drink of water from the village well and a ride on a horse and cart we had to sample the home-made wine and Tuica (lethal spirit distilled from plums). This had been made for the wedding. The farmhouse was well built and very cosy, and the hatch in the roof was the front door during the winter as the snow would be so deep at times it was the only form of exit. The car was loaded up with gallons and gallons of the home-made beverages and delivered to the hotel for the next day. The venue for the wedding breakfast was your normal hotel function room but had a strange looking pole attached to the dance floor!

Because we had a hire car, a very smart Volkswagen Polo, we were volunteered to be the chauffeur of the bride. A civil ceremony in the town hall, champagne on the very grand steps to celebrate (after Stefano had told the gypsies to vacate the spot), then it was off to their flat to watch Maria get dressed and made up, hair-do etc. by her maid of honour. She looked stunning, all the time being plied with sumptuous food, dangerous looking home-made wine and dancing. Next, we walked to the Coptic church for the religious bit. The priest sang the whole service while we stood up leaning against a wall with partitions on it. I looked towards Sarah and to my horror she was asleep. Alex gave her a dig in the ribs. "Wake up, Mummy." The home-made wine was taking effect.

Walking to the Palace of Culture for the photos was a welcome break from the constant eating and drinking, a great venue for your wedding pictures. Then it was off to the hotel for the reception, by design the hotel we were staying in. The next nine hours is a bit of a blur as we ate and danced, toasted and toasted again. It was Stefano and Maria's wedding, but we were the novelty and not left alone for a second. To get an English family to your wedding was a coup greater than being shot on Christmas Day.

Eventually we got back to Budapest and realised we had a day to spare. This was a bonus as it is a great city to explore and I recommend it to anybody. We booked a bus tour of the city, Buda on one side of the river Danube and Pest on the other. A boat trip up and down the great river gave us fantastic views of the elaborate Parliament palace. The goulash was fantastic.

Speaking of weddings far and wide, the next one was in Tenerife. The bar we call the office we drink in is called Cañada. (Which is an ancient name for stock trail in Spanish.)

The owners, Juan and Nuria's brother Diego, lives and works as a nurse in Santa de la Cruz, Tenerife. We had met him and his girlfriend, Desi many times at Christmas and during the summer holidays. In the Spring of 2009, an invitation was given to us to attend their wedding in the late autumn. In Tenerife. Times were hard and the recession was biting. Less people were coming on holiday and the building work was getting scarce.

"No, we can't go," I explained to our Spanish family. (We had been adopted by now.)

As if by magic a contract landed on my desk to build a house for a professor friend of ours, right here in Órgiva. He had retired from his post with the NHS and had a lump sum to invest in a house near to us that needed completely rebuilding. With income now secured for the foreseeable future we accepted the chance to go to Tenerife with our wonderful Spanish friends. Seventeen of us. I went ahead and booked our flights on the internet, and on explaining this to Juan an embarrassed expression appeared on his face.

"Could you book ours as well as we have never done anything like that before?"

I gathered all the necessary information and booked all of us on the same flight using my credit card. The total came to just under two thousand euros. The next day they gave me the cash. I tried to explain it was a credit card and I did not need the money for a couple of weeks. They insisted and shoved the wad into my hand.

As the wedding date got closer, I suggested we hired a mini bus to take us all to the airport. That was agreed, and Miguel did the booking. We all met early on a chilly November morning, the chatter was intense and the excitement tangible. After only half an hour we stopped for the obligatory coffee and a chance to light up.

At the airport it would have been easier to keep a flock of sheep going in the right direction. Security was a nightmare with wedding presents wrapped up and not knowing what was going to show up on the x-ray machines. Once through that obstacle it was off to the bar. Angeles took her tranquilisers too early and had to be nearly carried onto the plane, and the grandmother caused a scene when she got her knitting needles out. How she got those through security I don't know and the men were well into the beer. They all fell very quiet as we taxied and took off, but soon the chatter continued although with a slightly nervous edge to it. When the plane hit some turbulence, Angeles woke with a small squawk but soon was back in the land of nod again.

On landing in North Tenerife airport, nobody took any notice that Angeles was still asleep. Waking her up she looked very relieved to be on terra firma. The reception committee in arrivals was great to witness, lots of hugs and kisses. Hire cars were collected, and everybody loaded up. Now it was time for lunch, Tenerife style. Casa Tomas, Tegueste.

There were three kids in the party, all well behaved and enjoying the experience. Sarah and I were expecting to look at the menus because it all smelled and looked very good. But no, it was a set lunch and that was that. You try and tell three kids in England that you are going to eat what the grown-ups are having and there would be a riot. A delicious traditional meal of pork ribs, corn on the cob, boiled local spuds and a spicy mojo sauce all washed down with lots of good wine. Some light trading of Christmas lottery tickets took place, and no we can't pay our share for lunch.

The hotel was near Puerto la Cruz, Hotel Aguilas. Perched high on a hill overlooking the bay. Once check-in was complete and the plastic door keys explained, the kids were soon in the pool. We set off to town to get some supplies in. Dinner was a buffet style meal; I have never seen plates so full. I explained they could go back as many times as they liked. Breakfast the following day was similar, and when we arrived, they were sat there with toast and tomato spread. We turned up with a full English. The toast was ditched.

The day was organised and all we had to do was tag along. We were off to Santa Cruz to visit the bride and groom's apartment. After a tour of the flat and terrace refreshments were served, there was a rather explicit showing of the respective bride and groom's stag and hen parties. It got the girls' attention with hoots of laughter and grandma had to view it twice, and the word burro (donkey) was heard more than once.

Then lunch again, in a restaurant by the only golden sandy beach on the island. All the other beaches have black sand. The gold sand was imported from the Sahara Desert. Tenerife is a volcanic island, Mount Teide. Spain's highest mountain, standing at 3718 metres, it last erupted on November 18th, 1901. A hundred years ago.

The restaurant was called the Cofradia de Pescadores (the Brotherhood of the fishermen). A set menu of some of the best seafood I have ever eaten. The cheek flesh of the stone bass is said to have aphrodisiac properties! Again, not a murmur from the kids. After a long lunch, frantic trading of El Gordo tickets took place between the waiters and our party.

Back at the hotel I was explaining that the building had been used in a timeshare scam by a notorious gangster from Britain called John Palmer. He of the Brink's-Mat robbery. All the rooms had kitchens in them like an apartment hotel. A fortune had been made by him and a similar fortune had been lost by the people who invested in the scam.

Saturday arrived, the day of the wedding, an early evening service held in a beautiful old church near Desi's home village. I selected not to wear a tie as previous weddings we had attended I had been the only one to bother. Got it wrong. Back at the reception, the same hotel we were staying in, three times as many people were there as were at the church. That's consistent then! The reception went well with lots of eating, dancing, drinking and '"Que se besen" (kiss the bride) chanted by the guests. Desi and Diego were staying at the hotel for their nuptials, so brother Juan went and got the suitcases from the car. Bride, groom, suitcases, and ten more family members got into a lift to be elevated to the bridal suite. The lift broke between the eighth and ninth floor, overcrowded and with a particular lady suffering from claustrophobia who could not help relieving herself in the lift. We could hear the laughter from our room.

The next day at breakfast the giggling was still happening. We were to have a tour around Puerto de la Cruz. With the hire cars still decorated with ribbons and flowers we stopped at some traffic lights and a van driver looked at the cars and said, "Ah, a wedding." (Una boda.)

Sitting in the front with Juan, I stroked his stubbled face and said, "Beautiful, isn't he?" (Guapa.)

The lights turned green and he was off at the speed of lightning. The occupants of our car were splitting their sides with laughter. With the weekend drawing to a close there was time for one more lunch, then back on the plane. Angeles got her timing right and took her medication correctly. She is now a frequent flyer visiting her son in Stuttgart several times a year.

Weddings are getting more commercialised, with brides arriving in horse drawn carriages or vintage cars (Seats). Traditionally they walk to the church with their parents and siblings. Fireworks now welcome them out of the church instead of the barrage of rice and chickpeas. We went to one wedding when the reception could not start until the Spanish national football team had completed their important World Cup match. The bride was not impressed!

Neil, whose birthday party we gate-crashed with Miguel and Nuria, had an accident on the way to his work as a draughtsman in Bristol. He was riding his beloved Harley Davidson when a car pulled straight out in front of him giving him a hefty smack to the head and a broken pinkie. All seemed well until he had another accident and this time it was a broken leg. On further examination he had epilepsy through trauma. The original accident doing the damage. Their plan to join us in Órgiva had already started, they had bought a very nice plot of land with the idea to build a house on it. The news of Neil's condition accelerated their intentions to move and instead of building they bought a recently finished house with a manageable garden, close to Órgiva. Neil knew he would lose his driving license if he stayed in the UK and riding his motorbikes was his passion. Early 2005 Jackie and Neil moved to Spain.

With great excitement and plans to import old Harleys and renovate them their new life began. Small attacks of epilepsy would happen, petit mals, but with the right medication things were under control. The first Christmas came and although partying hard, all was well.

January the second a friend was banging on our bedroom window at five o'clock in the morning. "Neil is very ill you must come at once." On arrival at their house it was plain to see he had passed away. What on earth do we do now? I tried calling the police, but they did not understand me, so I was in a bit of a state. Eventually I found a Spanish friend who was having a very early morning coffee. I explained what had happened and he got onto things right away. Within ten minutes the police arrived, then a doctor and then a detective. An unexplained death at the age of fifty-two. Poor Jackie was in an awful state. Informing her two sons was not an easy thing to do either.

An autopsy was ordered, this delayed the funeral for a couple of days allowing friends and family to arrive from the UK. In Spain funerals take place very quickly, normally within twenty-hours from death. Don't hold your breath! This is because of the heat and no refrigeration also they believe the soul of the deceased needs protecting with constant chaperoning between the death and the internment.

Cremation was the choice and the nearest crematorium was in Granada. With everybody now present and accommodated in Órgiva the day arrived. I organised a mini-bus to take us all to the crematorium, not knowing what to expect and Jackie, or Neil for that matter, not wanting a religious ceremony we played some music and a friend read out The Lord is My Shepherd in the unloading bay of the premises. We witnessed the coffin enter the incinerator and then Jackie was asked which urn she would like. Gun metal grey, just like his Harley. We handed over the money, in cash, one thousand eight hundred euros and was asked if someone could wait to collect the urn when the ashes had cooled down sufficiently. All very business-like.

The wake was to take place at the bottom campsite bar. The Spanish do not have wakes; they are so worn out by the twenty-four-hour vigil they have no energy for drinking and toasting. A very sad story, only six months of his dream lived but he is always in our thoughts.

People who move abroad to live the dream seem to ignore the long-term and live for the short-term.

The Spanish have always regarded death as part of life, 'la va vida' they say when someone passes away, 'that's life'. In the past the deceased has always been laid out in the family's house but now we have a tanatorio (chapel of rest), the last house (ultima casa). Most towns have them now. The most expensive last hotel, in excess of three hundred euros a night. Insurance policies cover the cost. The church bell tolls a single chime for a male deceased and a two-bell chime for a female. The gathering in the tanatorio starts as soon as the death happens, dress is casual, vending machines supply refreshments and they all spill out onto the car park to smoke and discuss the price of olives. When the hearse leaves the last house, the mourners walk behind to the church. After the mass the coffin is taken by the hearse up through the town to the cemetery. As long as they can find the keys to the vehicle that is. A bar owner and friend passed away very young. We attended his funeral, and after the service the widow was offered a ride up to the cemetery which she accepted. The driver of the hearse got in to set off, but the keys were not in the ignition. We were watching from across the street. He checked his jacket, and he checked in the bar where he had had his coffee, but no keys. So, he rang his partner to bring over the spare set. Twenty minutes had now passed. The widow got out of the hearse and eureka she was sitting on them. A round of applause rippled through the waiting congregation. A Saw

Doctor's song, Same Old Town reminds me of the walk up the high street on the last journey. The cemetery consists of above ground boxes that the coffin slides into and then the front is sealed and eventually a granite plaque is stuck to the front with the epitaph inscribed on it. These days a photo is embossed on it as well. There is a lease agreement on these crypts and can last for five years to forty-nine years. Non-payment can mean eviction for the corpse. I don't know what happens to the remains then. In the film South of Granada, a funeral scene shows the coffin above the grave and then the bottom opens and drops the corpse into the ground. Very green, reusable coffins.

A Bulgarian guy called Gregory dropped down dead in one of the bars, he was only forty-two. As a Coptic Catholic the church would not let his funeral take place in the Catholic church, but Gregory often had a coffee with the assistant curate and a Coptic priest came up from Motril and took the service, all sang and it was very beautiful. The coffin was open and with lots of candles it made for a moving ceremony. Even Gregory's pain therapist was there with his dog. In English. Rest in Peace. R.I.P. In Spanish. Me One with Prayer. M.E.P.

Saint Barbara
December 4ᵗʰ

PATRON OF, ARCHITECTS, ARMOURERS, ARTILLERYMEN, SAILORS, brewers, firemen, fireworks makers, hatters, masons, mathematicians, military engineers, miners and smelters.

Saint Barbara was a virgin martyr in the third century AD. Her story is centred on her pagan father Dioscorus of Heliopolis, locking her up in a tower to protect her innocence and so that no man should see her great beauty. But a Christian disguised as a physician gained access to her and instructed her in the Faith. While Dioscorus was away at a war, he instructed an elaborate bathroom be built for her. Also, two windows were to be built into the tower. Barbara insisted a third window be constructed to honour the Holy Trinity.

On her father's return he noticed the third window and suspected the worst. He drew his sword to slay his daughter, but she escaped through the window and was transported to a cave in the mountains. An evil shepherd disclosed her whereabouts to her father. When he came to drag his daughter away the shepherd was turned to stone and his flock turned to locusts. When the father decapitated his daughter a bolt of lightning reduced him to a pile of ashes.

Saint Barbara looks after all that handle explosives, miners and gunners. (The French call a powder magazine a Sainte Barbe.) Also, her patronage of sailors inspired the Spanish mariners to name the difficult straits off the California coast, Santa Barbara.

We celebrate Santa Barbara in Órgiva due to the mining

connections. Must be a Cornish connection as well, because like I mentioned earlier in the book they always say, 'if you have a hole in the ground there is normally a Cornishman down it somewhere'. There is a barrio called Santa Barbara. With the fluorite mines open again and providing necessary employment Santa Barbara is a noisy affair. The miners hired a bar for the celebrations, you should have seen the scorch marks on the floor of the terrace. One year a miner lost a finger letting off rockets from his hand. The procession of Santa Barbara always took place in Tablones the headquarters of the mining operation but now the mass held in her honour is held in the church in Órgiva. On a visit to Cartagena, a Roman port and military city, we went into a church and in a niche the statue of Santa Barbara was displayed surrounded with artillery shells.

El Gordo: In search of The Fat One

AT THE END OF JUNE EACH year sheets of lottery tickets can be seen hanging up in bars and in shops, on sale on behalf of local organisations. This is the start of the annual Christmas Lottery. El Gordo. Sorteo Extraordinario de Navidad. People moan about Christmas starting too early in the UK, well beat that then!

The history of the oldest lottery in the world goes back to 1763 when King Carlos III used the proceeds to fund the Napoleonic War. El Gordo (the fat one) was first played in 1812 during the Spanish War of Independence in order to increase revenue for the State. The very first draw took place on March fourth. Since December eighteenth, 1812 the draw has been sung out by boys from the San Ildefonso School, Madrid, in a Gregorian chant style. In 1892 it became the lottery of Christmas. In 1984 the first girl to join in the singing of the draw was Monica Rodriguez. The draw now takes place on December twenty-second. It starts at eight-thirty am and lasts for four hours. It is televised to the whole nation; you cannot go anywhere without hearing the singing out of the numbers. Two large golden spherical cages are used. The large one contains small wooden balls with the ticket numbers on ranging from 00000 to 99999. The smaller one contains the 1,807 prizes. As each child sings out the ticket number, another child will sing out the prize the number has won.

To explain the system, I will keep it as simple as possible. Each number from 00000 to 99999 will be printed 160 to 180 times depending on what the Loterias y Apuestas del Estado decide on for this year's draw. So, each ticket is sold for twenty euros, and this number has been printed one hundred and sixty times. Tickets sold outside of the lottery shops, in bars, shops or even by an individual, carry a premium of two to three euros as a way of raising funds for the organisation that is represented by that number. As a member of the Cofradia de Dolores I sell ten tickets per year, the first foreigner to sell the Christmas lottery ticket in Órgiva. By adding three euros per ticket this will raise four hundred and eighty euros in donations to the organisation in question if all the tickets for the designated number are sold. There is nothing stopping an individual selling lottery tickets, often bars or other outlets will sell a number for their benefit. The mechanics garage I use will get a number from Valencia; I get a phone call from the secretary, "Would you like a ticket this year?" It's difficult to say no.

If one hundred and sixty individual people purchase a ticket, then the prize is divided by that number. Doing the sums, three thousand two hundred euros is generated by each number. Now multiply that by the number of tickets available and you come to a sum generated of thirty-two billion euros if all the tickets are sold. Seventy percent of this is prize money and sixty-four million to the first prize. Divided by one hundred and sixty tickets this equals four hundred thousand euros to the holders of each El Gordo ticket. Second prize is one hundred and twenty-five thousand each and third prize is fifty thousand each. Each subsequent prize tumbles down in value until the lowest amount of twenty euros. In other words, you get a refund.

This system of spreading the jackpot is a very sensible way of making people's lives more comfortable and not so rich that they become addicted to a lifestyle that is not in their comfort zone. A good analogy is; instead of a huge lump of butter on a small piece of toast suitable for one person to eat, the prize is the same size lump of butter but on a very large piece of toast cut into many portions for many people to enjoy. The way the tickets are sold in a localised area often effects a town or a village, a barrio or an organisation. Can you imagine say one hundred people winning four hundred thousand euros each and all living in the same town? It's not enough to blow on fast cars or extended holidays but it's enough to improve their homes and their way of life and lift up the trade in the locality.

An estimated three in four Spaniards and many foreigners purchase tickets in the lottery, with more than a million participants expected to take home some sort of prize. With odds as high as one in three, the lottery has continued to thrive. The premiums are added to the tickets to help all sorts of organisations, such as the town band, cofradias, football supporters' clubs, huntsmen's clubs, political parties and the church and can raise in excess of eighty million euros for good causes. The prize money has affected many people, in 1930 a garage owner and his mechanics won one thousand six hundred euros, a lot of money in those days. The garage owner lost all his staff, just like that. Even Franco's brother won a large prize. The Spanish guy who runs our acequia system won two hundred and fifty thousand euros three years ago. That was second prize, the ticket was bought from a village just down the road from us, he had two winning tickets. It didn't change him, he treated himself to a new car and paid off his mortgage. Spanish households spend about two-point five percent of their budget on lottery purchases and other forms of gambling, one of the highest in Europe. A Spanish friend described the El Gordo lottery as a sort of Christmas saving scheme with a chance of winning something big. Start buying in late June, say one a week, and by the time Christmas arrives you have bought twenty-five odd tickets. There is nothing stopping anybody from selling El Gordo tickets. Our local butcher has his number and sells them to his customers making three euros a ticket. If you are at a fiesta you will come across individuals selling lottery tickets. In cities you are forever pestered by lottery ticket sellers.

The investing begins so early as people going on holidays can buy tickets from different parts of the country not just for themselves but their mates as well. I often buy ten tickets from say, Cadiz or other places we visit. When I get back, I distribute them among my amigos and likewise they reciprocate when they return from their travels. It's a bit like kids swapping football stickers during World Cup tournaments. We were in Tarifa, early July. Outside the church the priest was selling El Gordo tickets on behalf of the church. Gospel of St. Mark 8.36: 'For what will it profit man if he gains the whole world and loses his own soul?'

Buying frenzies take place during the national holidays leading up to Christmas, October thirty-first and November first, and the long-bridged holiday of December sixth and the eighth. There is always a lot of visitors in town and the local tickets get snapped up. We went to a Spanish wedding in Tenerife in mid-November and after one lunch out came the tickets. Trading was brisk as the islanders like to get as many mainland tickets as possible. Manolo who owns and runs the local builders' merchants is keen on his lottery, he asks all the reps that visit him to purchase tickets. I was in there once near Christmas and a recorded delivery arrived, it was a lottery ticket. Businesses use the tickets as a thank-you to loyal customers. As the saying goes, you have to be in it to win it, and an estimated thirty-six million people will hold a ticket for next Christmas.

Leading up to Christmas you might notice large baskets or hampers of goodies behind the bar of your local. Fancy baskets full of bottles, chocolates, turron, jamon, salamis and other such delicacies of the festive season. There will be a sheet numbered from 0 to 99 and a space to write your name in at a cost. The last two numbers of El Gordo will win you this intriguing prize. It's worth entering just to investigate the contents if you are lucky enough. A local guy, larger than life managed one year to get his lucky number on the sheet of three bars and ended up with enough goodies to last him and his family for half the year.

Closely following El Gordo is El Nino. This draw was first established in 1942, dedicated to children and takes place on January sixth, Epiphany, in the Teatro Falla, Cadiz. Again, the tickets cost twenty euros and again charitable organisations can sell tickets to raise funds. A lot less tickets are printed but it still generates a prize fund of eight hundred and forty million euros, with 22,687 prizes and a first prize of two hundred thousand euros handed to each of the hundred lucky ticket holders.

There are many weekly lotteries held in Spain and all look very confusing when entering a lottery shop. I will attempt to explain how to play them, invest and win!

El Gordo de la Primitiva. This is a weekly lottery drawn on a Sunday lunchtime. You have a coupon with two grids on it. One grid has numbers from 1 to 54 and the other has numbers 0 to 9. Players have to pick five numbers from the first grid and one number in the second. Tickets can be bought from Monday through to Saturday in over 12,000 different locations throughout Spain and cost 1.50 euros per grid. First prize is a perfect match 5+1, second 5+0, third 4+1 and so on totalling 8 prize categories. The first prize is a guaranteed five million euros. This can accumulate if no match is made, often leading to huge bonus prizes.

Bono Lotto. Draws are held on Monday, Tuesday, Wednesday and Friday. This draw was first introduced in 1988. The aim of the game was to provide frequent draws at affordable prices. Players have to match 6 numbers from 1 to 49. During the draw a 7th additional number is drawn, the so-called complimentary which is used as a 5 + 1 winning category. A single line costs .50 cents but the minimum investment is 1 euro. 55% of the income is allocated as prizes. The jackpot starts at 400,000 euros and rolls over each time the jackpot is not won. The largest jackpot ever won was 8 million in 2017. Winnings over 2,500 euros are subject 20% tax, this was introduced in 2013.

Spanish Football Quiniela. This is very similar to the good old football pools in the UK and dates back to the early 1970's. The lottery game is based on the results of certain football matches pre-printed on the betting slip. There are fifteen matches and all you have to do is predict the outcome of fourteen of the matches by home win, draw or away win. The fifteenth you need to predict the exact number of goals scored by each team. There are four options. 1. 0- Zero goals 2. 1- One goal 3. 2- Two goals 4. M- Three or more goals. Each Quiniela ticket has eight betting columns costing 50 cents each, a minimum of two columns need to be filled in to be validated. Prizes are paid on ten predictions and upwards. Ten out of fifteen will win you 9 euros.

The Thursday lottery is a national weekly game, six million tickets are printed, and cost three euros and the coupon consists of five numbers and a serial number. Match all the numbers and six hundred thousand euros is yours, second prize is sixty thousand euros.

The Saturday lottery is again a national weekly game, ten million tickets are printed and cost six euros. The top prize is one million euros. There are some special draws where the tickets cost more. Second prize is two hundred and fifty thousand and third is fifty thousand euros. With all Spanish lotteries there are many smaller prizes. They work backwards. If you get the last number drawn, then you are reimbursed with your initial stake and so on. This system is used in local raffles, using the ONCE draw to determine the winner of such prizes. No doubt about a fix!

The lottery shop is the only visible gambling establishment on the high street in Spain. Compare this to the UK high street where you can choose from four or five turf accountants all in a row. Gone are the days of the smoke-filled dens full of pensioners having their daily punt and catching up on the local gossip. The modern-day bookies are now smoke free. Even failed betting slips are put in the bins instead of strewn across the floor and free tea and coffee are offered. Huge slot machines (now called gaming machines) promise massive pay-outs and have been the ruin of many an addict. The study of form of both dog and horse is a great hobby to have and sensible retirees enjoy the daily chance with a set budget to lighten their day. The lessons having been learnt from many years of investment, successfully or not. There is a lot of advertising on Spanish media about the betting apps you can obtain on your phone to bet on football etc, but the Spanish high streets being filled with brightly lit betting shops is not going to happen as the government relies heavily on the income from their beloved lotteries.

The lottery outlets are again an historical franchise handed out to loyal supporters of the cause. Generations grow up taking on the business. Once, on entering my local shop the wind outside was bitter and the lady had a bunch of envelopes covering the serving hatch. I asked what the envelopes were for, having noticed them before.

"We keep regular clients' tickets safe. Each week we know what they play and place the coupons in these envelopes, then they come in once a week and pay. It saves the tickets getting lost or washed in the washing machines, also the wife won't find out if the husband has a win."

"That's a bit sneaky," I replied.

"Oh, the women do it as well you know!"

The Euro millions draw obviously has a massive market with nine countries involved. It was established in 2004 and attracts lots of players. The prospect of winning massive pay-outs for first prize and very little for second puts a lot of people off this game. Imagine a roll over for eight weeks, the money accumulated by the organisers over this period of time is obscene and then to get so close to winning and missing by one number! Recently a roll over led up to a jackpot of one hundred and twenty-four million euros. Just for a laugh I entered six of the seven winning numbers. Second prize was three thousand euros. Not the Spanish way is it, toast and butter!

On your travels around Spain and in your town, village, cities and Ikea stores you cannot help but notice people selling lottery tickets for an organisation called ONCE. Organizacion Nacional de Ciegos Espanoles. Established in 1938 it describes itself as a 'large dose of energy'. The main purpose of this organisation is to provide employment and social inclusion of disabled people right across Spain.

It started with the blind and partially sighted. They have been selling the coupon since May eighth, 1939. ONCE now employ over eighty thousand people selling tickets and another fifty-three thousand in administration. Every day of the week you can buy a ONCE coupon. There are special draws for Christmas, Father's Day, Mother's Day, Mid-summer and the eleventh of November. The vendors of the tickets now wear green and yellow waistcoats to attract your attention, Norwich City football colours.

In its eightieth year of existence the organisation will be celebrating a system of social benefits for the blind and visually impaired that has no equivalent anywhere else in the world. The money raised by the coupon sellers goes directly to people that need it. ONCE is overseen by a board of patrons and a general council of democratically elected members. They have built educational centres to guarantee good training from the bottom, giving rise to cultural initiatives, such as libraries with Braille, audio support and rehabilitation. Spain always does well in the para-Olympics mainly due to the funding from ONCE. They sponsored a cycle team from 1989 to 2003. To become a coupon seller, you must have Spanish citizenship, your best corrected visual acuity must be equal to or less than 0.1 (1/10 on the wecker scale) or have a visual field of less than ten degrees or less.

The coupon costs one euro fifty cents from Monday to Thursday, three euros on a Friday and two euros on Saturday and Sunday. The prizes vary but the one that would be nice to win would be Saturday or Sunday. Seventy-two thousand euros per year for twenty-five years. I know somebody who won this, but the most I have won was five hundred euros. To collect such a prize just go to any Spanish bank. They read it with a bar code reader and ask if you want it put into your account or cash. Winning is pleasant but knowing you are directly helping by making a contribution is a reward in itself. Scratch cards are now available as well, which can cause instant amusement in a bar full of happy people.

Everybody knows how healthy the black economy is in Spain, achieving permanent employment is very difficult and becoming self-employed is expensive. The best way for the government to collect revenue is through the lottery. Poor man's tax. That started in 1796.

One lottery you should check. Did you opt out of SERPS since 1988, you might have a surprise around the corner. I did!

Other Celebrated Days
Day of the Constitution (National Holiday)
December 6th

FRANCO RULED SPAIN FOR FORTY YEARS as a military dictator, but after his death in 1975 the country slowly returned to a democracy under the leadership of King Juan Carlos 1. The Constitution then repealed all the fundamental laws of the realm as well as other major historical laws and every pre-existing law that contradicted what the Constitution stood for. December the 6th was chosen as the day to celebrate the event as it was close to the day of the Immaculate Conception, to give the Spanish people a holiday before the Christmas celebrations begin.

Immaculate Conception
(National Holiday)
December 8ᵗʰ

PATRON OF ARMY CHAPLAINS, CLOTH WORKERS, coopers, upholsterers, USA, & Zaire.

The Immaculate Conception does not refer to the conception of Jesus Christ, which is known as the Incarnation. Do not confuse the two as you will get some very angry nuns at your heels. This major holy day honours Mary's own conception in the womb of her mother, Saint Anne. It seems that Mary's parents did not do the deed, that is to say they took no pleasure in the act whatsoever. So, Mary was born with no original sin and thus became a fit vessel to carry God's only son. This day was Mother's Day in Spain until 1965 now it is the first Sunday in May.

Day of Columbus (National Holiday)
Hispanic Day ~Santa Pillar
October 12th

OUR LADY OF THE PILLAR (The Blessed Virgin Mary). A vision of the Virgin was witnessed by the Apostle James the Greater as he was praying on the banks of the River Ebro, near Zaragoza, Hispania in AD forty. The wooden image of Santa Pillar is enshrined at the Basilica of Our Lady Pillar, Zaragoza. The feast day lasts nine days and is known as Fiestas del Pillar in the area of Zaragoza. It is also the day of the Civil Guard and Columbus Day. Thus, a national holiday for the whole of Spain.

Pope Clement XII allowed the celebration of the feast of Our Lady of the Pillar all over the Spanish Empire in 1730, as the date coincides with the discovery of the Americas. The Lady was named as patroness of the Hispanic world.

This day also coincides with the day in 1492 when land was first sighted on Christopher Columbus's first voyage. The name of Día de Hispania was introduced on the ninth of January 1958 and decreed a national holiday.

The Day of Andalucía
February 28th

THIS DAY MARKS THE ANNIVERSARY OF the referendum held in 1980 to declare Andalucía as an autonomous community in Spain.

In Órgiva the natural products of Andalucía that feed us are celebrated with the traditional breakfast of toast, tomatoes and olive oil for everybody in the main square, donated by many generous businesses and organised by the town hall. Also, local politicians may present people with certificates and medals for services to the community.

Saint Patrick
March 17th

SAINT PATRICK IS CELEBRATED IN ALBONDON, but also anywhere where there are Irish people about or in any bar that sells Guinness. Draught Guinness was not sold anywhere in Órgiva until El Rincon got a pump in and a sign outside announcing the fact. A couple of weeks before Saint Patrick's Day we went in for a pint (again pints were not normally served in the area, it was a tubo or a caña).

"Two pints please, Jose." By this time, we had shown Jose how to pour a pint of the black stuff. Two delivered and two stickers. "What's this?" I enquired. Collect six stickers and you get a free T-shirt in preparation for Saint Patrick's Day. Now, we all like a challenge, I forget how many T-shirts we ended up with. As we got closer to the day, we asked Jose what he was planning for the evening of the 17th. Monday the 17th.

The answer, "We don't open on Mondays!"

"Well you are open on this Monday."

We organised the music, spread the word around and had a fantastic night. The place was rammed, and we drank him dry of Guinness.

Saint Joseph
March 19th

PATRON OF CARPENTERS, FATHERS, HOUSE HUNTERS, Belgium, Austria, Mexico and Peru.

Joseph was the foster father of Jesus, slightly upset that his wife had become pregnant without his input (so to speak) until an angel explained the plan. Joseph and his wife remained celibate during their married life and this is a cornerstone of the Catholic faith. One of his emblems is the crutch which symbolises his supposed impotence. He is also the patron of a happy death. Pope Pius XI in 1933 proclaimed him patron of those who combat Communism. Pope Pius XII's proposed his feast day be on May 1st as a counterdemonstration to the socialists' godless May Day.

The closest town to celebrate Saint Joseph is the seaside town of La Herradura. It's a wonderful celebration in a great Spanish resort. Unspoilt and still very Spanish.

Motril, Earthquake Day
January 13ᵗʰ 1804

MOTRIL, A TOWN OF 66,000 ON the coast and the only place in Europe where sugar cane was grown, suffered a major earthquake on this day and the scared townsfolk turned to their saints. They paraded Jesus Nazareno and the Virgin of the Cabeza around the town and the shaking stopped. So, still to this day the parades take place, along with a fiesta of course.

Halloween and the day of All Saints

HALLOWEEN WAS HARDLY CELEBRATED WHEN WE first arrived, now thanks to the American influence and the Chinese emporium (Halloween costumes) you can't escape it. It's the feast day of Saint Quentin. It's now so popular they have a week of fear. It was delayed for two days due to the inclement weather a few years ago. Is that why the famous American prison was called San Quentin?

The Feast of All Saints
November 1ˢᵗ

THIS DAY IS A NATIONAL HOLIDAY in Spain, the day flower sellers have their busiest day. Everybody visits the graves of their loved ones, a sombre day. It was the first day of the Celtic calendar, the festival of Samain. It seemed an opportunity occurred when the worlds of the living and the dead had a chance to mix for a day and a night. It's a feast for all saints known or unknown.

The Final Course

AS WITH ANY GOOD MEAL OR journey there has to be an end, and so to the last chapter of this book. After two decades of hard work, something new to learn every day and the gamble we put in place paying off, it is getting close to the time to realise our assets. Our own pension plans. My hip has been replaced again and what with other aches and pains, not just with me, but Sarah is suffering as well with arthritis, our time to retire approaches.

The British Government extending the time when ladies will receive their pension from the age of sixty to sixty-seven (my theory of marrying an older woman being a gamble lost!) reinforces our approach that managing our own pension fund was and is a correct decision. Paying national insurance as part of your pension planning cannot anymore be a guaranteed result. When a government can just move the goal posts due to their own financial bad management and then take it out on their own citizens, it is not correct or even legal.

Going back to the preface of this book I mentioned my father was not a gambler although he invested heavily into a private pension fund. Now this is a gamble taken on by both parties, the investor and the assurance company. If the investor lives to be a ripe old age, then the company supplying the annuity has to keep paying out, but if the investor (pensioner) dies early then all of that hard-earned cash goes into their pot. A family asset lost for good.

The other option is to manage your own pension fund. Spread the risk but keep your investments as part of your family's assets. Property, stamps, coins, fine wine or art are some of the options, not forgetting an annual income will be needed. Also, retiring early so you can enjoy relatively good health to do the things you want to, the trips, adventures, visiting friends and following hobbies you never had time for (like trying to write a book).

The first of our assets to be sold were the guesthouses, they had done us proud. Appreciation, income and a focus on living in Spain. We feel we got away lightly as the laws on letting country property to tourists have tightened considerably and earning a decent income has diminished. Selling a property in Spain is an expensive business, as the appreciation has slowed down and making a profit on property has diminished. In the old days under-declaring was the norm, and a big fat envelope of cash was handed over in front of the notary during the signing.

During the years of letting we have come across many wonderful and interesting people. Shula Archer and her husband Brian Aldridge stayed, as well as Peter Skelleren. One guest who was helping her husband search for his birth mother actually located Sarah's birth mother in Canada. Another guest from Barcelona, a teacher, was amazed by the local accent. She described it as if people swallowed the beginning and the end of their words. This reminds me of an incident at the builders' merchants. My neighbour, Jesus had been doing some fencing and on top of his car were some fencing poles he was returning. In his very rural accent, he was trying to tell Manolo what he was doing. Manolo did not understand him and looked at me, so I told him he was returning six fencing poles. I was now interpreting Spanish to Spanish. (Only because I saw what he had on top of his car.)

Órgiva is a revolving door, foreign people come, live the dream, stay a while and then return to their native land for many reasons. The most potent force that draws them away is of impending grandchildren that will need love and caring for as many new young parents both have jobs and paying for child care is beyond the economic reasons for working.

Living in such a wonderful place makes it a pleasure to return from holiday, either by road, plane or train. The first sight of the valley nestling in mountains makes your heart sing.

Reluctantly, Órgiva is becoming more northern European. There is an English shop selling popular brands that some people can't do without and a supermarket in town stocks foreign foods. One Christmas they stocked Christmas crackers, but the owner placed them in the biscuit section. He was alarmed when told they were small bombs full of plastic rubbish. Health food shops exist and do a great trade. The high street is still vibrant, no Lidl or Aldi here. As people walk past you say hello and they say goodbye, is that where the Beatles got the lyric from?

Reflecting on the changes we have experienced over our time here would be similar to most parts of the modern world. Young people don't wear wrist watches, telephone directories have disappeared, television scheduling is a mess as programmes can be watched at any time, and people wander about with ear plugs in their ears and switch off from the world around them not knowing if they are listening to their phone or their camera. In some city's lights are being installed on the pavement to warn people of lampposts and other obstructions they might walk into. Bluetooth connection is a fantastic invention, named after a Danish king who united Denmark. Harald Bluetooth, 935 to 985. The symbol is made up of Nordic runes, the Bluetooth technology unites different devices under its rule. Actual conversations by mobile phone have decreased and now messages are norm as a pastime even if you have nothing to say. Next, they will have permanent masks on their faces so they can't smell the essence of the street. Mobile phones can open hotel doors and you can even buy beer with them (dangerous). Floppy discs have gone, VHS disappeared, DVD's, CD's, it's all streamed. On the positive E Books are losing popularity and traditional books are back in favour (I say optimistically). If you don't have a Google account with numerous passwords and pin numbers, then a simple purchase of a laptop is impossible. The fear of getting hacked and your cloud being burst is an everyday worry. Following people vaping is like being in a permanent fog as smoking tobacco gets the elbow. People fly by on their electric push bikes with no effort at all.

It feels like when we arrived in Órgiva the town was in the fourth division; I would say promotion has happened, but we are still not in the premiership.

Writing this book is a gamble, and Sarah will kill me if I don't sell a few copies as all the time I spent researching and writing this book, the outside work on the finca has been neglected.

Orgiva is an essence you cannot bottle, preserve it or replicate it. You just have to experience it and remember the occasion. I was asked by a friend, "How did you know your move would work out so well?"

My reply was, "We didn't, it was a punt." What's life without taking a risk?

Órgiva is such a vibrant, multi-cultural, alternative society. Art, music, authors, many different holistic healing therapies and exercise programmes. Prana energy healers, Ayurvedic clinic, Chakra balance healing, Acupressure, Acupuncture, Aromatherapy, Massage, Indian head massage, Meditation, Qigong, Reflexology, Reiki, Tai Chi and many different Yogas (even tantric sex courses). Every day is a fancy-dress day in town, and you witness people wearing all sorts of attire from kilts, jellabiya, cravats, sports jackets, top hats to baggy trousers. There are musicians busking, jugglers juggling, one Thursday (market day) someone had a full-size piano in the square playing great music. Different schooling is available, Steiner and Montessori. We could be twinned with Glastonbury or Totnes or even both. As mentioned before, we have many bars in the town, all different, one described by a friend as, "In the morning it's like the Black Pearl and the afternoon the Glastonbury music festival."

With the uncertainty of Brexit, a lot less chancers are giving it a go. The question all the Spanish ask is why? They call it CONALTH. Confused Other Nations About Leaving the Handouts.

Whatever you do in your life it's your energy, your journey, your chance.

Glossary

Acequia	Irrigation channel
Aciete	Olive oil
Agua	Water
Aguilla	Eagle
Ajo Blanco	Garlic and Almond soup (cold)
Alberca	Water store
Alpujarra	Mountainous region south of Granada
Apoda	Nickname
Automino	Self-employed
Ayuntamiento	Townhall
Bachillerato	European A levels
Barra	Fat baguette
Barranco	Dry river bed, gully
Bascule de Puente	Weigh Bridge
Belen	Nativity scene
Bocaadillo	Another fat baguette
Bomberos	Firefighters
Bota	Leather wine bag
Bovedillas	Roof blocks
Brevas	Early figs
Calentador	Gas water heater
Caliente	Hot

Calle	Street
Camino	Road
Campesino	Country person
Canguro	Babysitter
Caña	Cane or Bamboo
Capacha	Circular mat used in olive oil production
Capriotes	Pointed hats worn at Easter time
Carajillo	Coffee with a spirit added
Carcoma, Hylotrupes Bajulus	Wood eating beetle
Carretera	Road
Casera	Home made
Casita	Small house
Cenicero	Ashtray
Chirenguito	Beach bar
Chispa	Spark
Choetes	Rockets with no colour
Choto	Cooked goat stew
Chumba	Cactus
Cintas	Ribbon´s
Comadrona	Mid-wife
Compra Venta	Buying and selling contract
Concurso	Competition
Copa	Wine glass
Coraza	Pointed hat
Corredor	Runner, agent
Cortijo	Farmhouse
Costa	The coast or dangerous local wine
Costaleros	People that carry the saints at celebrations
Cristo	Christ
Cuantro Vientos	Four winds

Cuatro latas	Four tins
Cuba libre	Spirit drink with a mixer
Denuncia	To report someone
Derecha	Right
Despacio	Slow down
El Brazo	Arm
Embutidos	Preserved pork products, salami etc.
Esquinas	Corners
Estancos	Tobacconists
Estrellas	Stars
Expiracion	End
Extranjero	Foreigner
Ferreterria	Iron mongers
Finca	Farm or plot of land with productive plants
Fino	Sherry
Frio	Cold
Gaña	Gain
Golondrinas	Swallows
Granadina	Someone from Granada
Gualalfeo	Ugly river
Guapa	Beautiful
Guiris	Northern Europeans nickname
Hecho	Made
Heilo	Ice
Hermanadads	Brotherhoods
Higos	Second crop of figs
Hogueras	Bonfires
Hola	Hello
Huesos	Bones
Hueveros	Egg people
Igualmente	Equal to you

Impuestos	Tax
Inocentes	Innocents
Izquierda	Left
Jamon	Air dried ham
La Abuela	Grandmother
La va vida	That's life
Launa	Grey magnesium roof water proofer
Leña	Firewood
Limpio	Clean
Longaniza	Red sausage
Madrinas	Godmothers
Manchada	Weak coffee
Medioambiente	Environment agency
Membrio	Quince
Merienda	Snack for children around 5pm
Migas	Bread crumb savoury dish
Modelo	Model
Morcilla	Black pudding
Mucho	Lots
Musto	Grape juice
Noche Buena	Christmas eve
Nota simple	Statement of debt on a property
Obra Minor	Small building job
Pancello con cruz	Hot cross bun
Pappa Noel	Father Christmas
Pavo	Turkey
Pero	But
Pinchitos	Spiced pork on a skewer
Pipote	Clay pot for keeping drinking water cool
Polvo	Dust
Porron	Glass drinking vessel with a spout

Pozo Negro	Black hole for sewage
Propina	Tip for a waiter
Puntales	Prop for holding up a roof
Que se Besen	Kiss the bride
Quirofano	Operating theatre
Rebano	Flock of sheep
Rejuneos	Bull fighting on horse back
Rentoy	Spanish card game
Saeta	Gypsy woman who sang at the foot of the cross
Secadero	Ham drying building
Segurena	Spanish breed of sheep
Semaforo	Traffic lights
Sendaro	Walking path
Seprona	Environmental branch of the Guardia Civil
Sobre	Envelope
Tanatoria	Funeral parlour
Tapas	Food with a drink
Tersio	Third of a litre of beer in a bottle
Tracas	Firework bangers
Trafico	Traffic branch of the Guardia Civil
Traje de Luz	Matadors suit of light
Tubo	Size of a glass of beer
Vamos	Lets go
Vendimia	Grape harvest
Viga	Roof beams
Yata	The end (local word)

Acknowledgements

I WOULD LIKE TO THANK THE many people that have provided so much information without even being aware of the fact. David Atkinson from the Racing Post for the initial proof reading. Jayne Skellet for trying to make me into some sort of scribe. Chris Stewart for his encouragement. Sarah and David Luddington from Mirador Publishing. My daughter for the cover design and IT support. Mort Rosenblum for his book; Olives, the Life and Lore of a Noble Fruit and The Saint-a-Day Guide by Sean Kelly and Rosemary Rodgers. All the wonderful tolerant Spanish friends that have looked after us during these years of discovery. Last and no means least my wife Sarah for her patience and putting up with strange messages being sent to her as memories were re-ignited with the help of a beer or two.